Pipe Dreams

Alan Aldridge burst upon the creative world of 1960s London, just like the Beatles for whom he worked. His imaginative designs and intoxicating, colourful images captured the dreams and hallucinations of a generation in *The Beatles Illustrated Lyrics*, a deluxe edition of which was published in 2013; on album covers for The Who, Cream and Elton John; on the notorious Chelsea Girls poster for Andy Warhol; and, as an Art Director on innovative covers for Penguin Books.

In the 1970s Aldridge produced bestselling children's' books including *The Butterfly Ball* and *The Peacock Party*, plus the logo for the Hard Rock Café. He moved into animation in Los Angeles, working on film and TV projects, as well as designing for bands including Incubus and Tears For Fears. He calls himself a 'graphic entertainer' and his body of work confirms that label. He has published twelve books, including *The Penguin Book of Comics*, *Phantasia*, a novel – *The Gnole* – and an illustrated memoir, *The Man With Kaleidoscope Eyes*.

T0352482

Pipe Dreams

ALAN ALDRIDGE

SPELLBINDING
M E D I A

LONDON

Published by Spellbinding Media 2014

First published in Great Britain in 2014 by

Spellbinding Media
Third Floor, 111 Charterhouse Street, London, EC1M 6AW
www.spellbindingmedia.co.uk
facebook.com/spellbindingmedia
twitter.com/sbmediauk

Spellbinding Media Ltd Reg. No. 08482364
A CIP catalogue record for this book is available
from the British Library.
ISBN 978-1-909964-06-8

Typeset in Plantin by ForDesign, London
Printed and bound by TJ International Ltd, Padstow, Cornwall

"This is a work of creative non-fiction"
ALAN ALDRIDGE

Author's Note

In *Pipe Dreams*, I revisit my early years. Part of this book is set in London's gritty East End 1960s gang culture. You may find some of the scenes, which I describe to the best of my recollection, shocking. I have chosen to include them because they are based on actual experiences, even if I have fictionalised some of the characters.

Chapter One

I'd known Tony 'the Greek' Lazarus since I was a kid. He was three years older than me and always in trouble with the police. We went to the same school as each other, on the Roman Road.

Funnily enough, we both shared the dubious distinction of having been expelled at the age of thirteen, me for absenteeism (I preferred the billiard hall) and Tony for something much more spectacular. During a maths exam, Basil Baines – a much-feared cane-wielding teacher – had accused Tony of cheating.

Not one of Basil's best ideas.

Tony attacked him with a fury. Every finger on his huge hands was heavily ringed, each ring honed with razor-sharp edges. He used them to pound and chop into the meat of Basil's face, to the delight and cheers of the other pupils.

When it was over, Basil's eyes, ears, nose and teeth had been rearranged to resemble some ghastly Francis Bacon painting; as for Tony, he got hauled away by the police to be detained at Her Majesty's Pleasure for a six-month stretch in Borstal, a detention centre for young offenders.

"Borstal's the best school I ever went to," Tony said, boasting upon his return to Bethnal Green. "Learned more about villainy in five minutes there than what I did in all the rest of my life," he added, ungrammatically.

Back on the streets Tony formed a gang of young thugs. At the age of fourteen he was wearing Teddy Boy drapes and brothel creepers as he sauntered along on his way towards living a life of crime and ever-escalating violence.

"For starters I got into petty theft, nicking cheap jewellery from department stores. Necklaces, earrings, they sell real quick down Petticoat Lane. Plus, give a bird a cheap bit of cut glass and call it a brooch, she'll do anyfin' if you know what I mean."

I was sitting with Tony and the boys at a marble-topped table in G. Kelly's Eel Pie Shop on Roman Road. Tony was giving us his daily dose of verbal diarrhoea. He made curious animal mating noises mixed with a lot of nudge-nudges and wink-winks to make sure that we'd know what he meant.

"My next career move was robbin' old ladies," he went on. "See, the old man, 'e works 'ard all week down the docks and, on Friday night, comes home and hands over 'is pay packet to the missus. Sure enough, every Saturday morning, you'll find these little ol' mums waddling around the market, buying food for the week and flashing their fat little purses full of pound notes.

"I mean, they were asking to be robbed. And I obliged. Next I moved in on cars, easy to rob – and they don't yell and scream like the old gals. Amazing what people leave in their cars. I've nicked radios; portable gramophones; wallets; sets of golf clubs; telescopes; TVs… You name it. One time, we nicked a 'earse parked on City Road."

He paused.

"Actually," he began, "thinking back, it weren't too clever. We sees this 'earse parked with no driver, he's probably gone for a cuppa tea. So Terry says 'earses could be worth a few bob, so let's nick it. Well, we all thought without finking it'd be a giggle, so I pulls up the Zephyr, out jumps Nobby, hotwires the funeral vehicle and off we go.

"We 'eads straight to The Wheatsheaf pub on Bethnal Green Road. The landlord, Charlie Copsey, is one of the biggest fences in the East End. He'll buy just about anyoldfin. We pulls the two motors up in the pub's car park and mosey inside to find Charlie. Well, he ain't there – gone down the bank to deposit his week's earnings... And I'm thinkin', I wish I'd known that, I would've come earlier and mugged 'im myself, made a quick bundle.

"Anyway, we all have a quick 'alf-pint and head back to the motors to wait. Well, when we gets outside did we do a bloody double-take? Don't we just. The 'earse is gone. That's the trouble with the bleedin' East End: can't turn your back on nuffin' for five minutes, not without some thievin' rascal stealin' it. Nobody's got any effics anymore...

"Well, guess what? I sees a neat little ol' man sitting calmly in the back seat of my Zephyr. Bleedin' cheek, I think. 'Hey you,' I yells. 'What d'you fink you're up to?' Geezer don't move a muscle. So, I'm really pissed off. I goes and yanks him out and I notices something.

"He's dead. Dead as a bleedin' doornail.

"I can't believe the stroke some cheeky bastard has pulled: not only nickin' the 'earse but 'avin' 'ad the fuckin' liberty to take the coffin and leave us with the corpse. Then Nobby, who's always quick on the uptake, says, 'Maybe the old gent needs a stiff drink. Get it? Stiff drink... For a stiff.'

"So, Jimmy puts his shades on the old man and me and Nobby lift him up by the arms – he's as light as a feather – and, giggling our 'eads off, carries him straight into The Wheatsheaf and props him up between us right at the bar."

Tony leaned forward now, drawing us further into the story.

"So now the barman asks us, 'What'll it be?' and I orders four 'alves of bitter for me and the boys and a pint of wallop for the old man, cos he's dead thirsty. And we all crack up laughing.

"Nobby chimes in again, 'And don't stiff us on the change!' and so we all fall about, fit to bust. The barman tells us to quiet it down, so I'm thinking about whether I should knuckle-sandwich 'im, when an old girl gets up out of her chair, all annoyed-like, and comes over and confronts the stiff.

"She says, 'Herbert? Is that you?' and I mean, blimey – she knew 'im! 'Herbert,' she goes on, 'Elsie said you were dead, you passed away yesterday. I'm goin' to your funeral tomorrow, so what you doin' 'ere, drinking this early, 'anging about with this rough lot?'

"She tut-tuts her disapproval of me and Nobby. 'Really Herbert,' she adds, 'and wearing those stupid sunglasses.'

"Knock me down with a feather, if the first time in my life I'm at a loss for words and I'm wondering how much time inside I'd get for abducting a dead stiff. But I've always had the gift of the gab and so my mind comes to the rescue. 'This ain't Herbert, darlin,' I says. 'It's Percy – Herbert's twin

4

brother. He's deaf, dumb and blind, love. 'E's down 'ere from Newcastle to attend his brother's funeral.'

"Well, she was flabbergasted and she snorts, 'Herbert never told me nothing about no twin brother.'

"Right then, as if to save the day, the corpse lets out this huge fart. It went on forever and stunk like rotting cabbage. What a stink! Everyone in the bar was stumbling outside for fresh air and the barman's yelling at us to get the hell out.

"So we does. We dump Herbert in the back of the car and burn rubber out of there. As we're driving along, we figure we'd just bung the body out someplace, but thought that would be kind of undignified, plus Nobby said it would really piss God off.

"Again, my mind comes up with a great idea as to 'ow we can save the situation: we takes Herbert to the Emergency Room at Bethnal Green Hospital. The place, as usual, was chaotic: people staggering around with knife wounds, blood everywhere, kids crying, pregnant mums screaming…

"It was perfect. We just walks right in and props Herbert up against the cigarette machine, which was easy cos he was all stiff with rigatoni, and out we strolls. Mission accomplished."

Tony roared with laughter. "So boys, there you have it: Lesson Number Two of the Gospel According to Saint Tony."

We all sat blank-faced, not sure what Lesson Two was. Or Lesson One, for that matter. But nobody said a dicky bird, everyone anxious to go home.

But it wasn't to be. Tony rolled on, onto Lesson Number Three.

"Another time I broke into a big Humber. Inside stunk like a bleedin' harem: sickly perfume mixed with Turkish cigarettes. There was ornate rugs on the floor. I'm thinking, it's either a drug dealer's or a pimp's car, so I give it a real once-over and under the front seat – bingo! I finds an ornate vase, so I grabs it, along with a beautiful pair of leather gloves, a box of one hundred Abdulla cigarettes and about thirty pairs of nylon stockings.

"When I gets to the Como Café, I take a good look at the vase. It's real heavy and the top is sealed with cloth and wax. All very intriguing. Then, on the side, I sees this little brass plate that says *Maria Ahjahdian 1872 to 1962*.

"Damn, it's a bloody cremation urn.

"So I sells the vase and the ashes I dumped, except for maybe a gram, which I put into a pharmaceutical vial to 'ave a giggle with cos, later, I'm over at Nobby's, my strong-arm man. We're playing cards. I pulls out my little vial and Nobby's eyes light up 'cos he's a real pig when it comes to drugs. I lays a big line on a mirror, 'e rolls up a pound note and snorts the whole lot up 'is hooter in double-quick time.

"The muscle-brained twat is standing there, sniffing and smiling, saying it was really good shit. What a laugh! So I empties the vial onto the mirror and he's down again, sniffing it up like a pig in shit, then standing about grinning ear-to-ear, and tells me, 'Tony, great smack, man. Whoa. Just... Great!'

"What an actor. He flops onto the sofa, grinning like a bloody baby, his eyes dancin' about and lookin' all glassy. So I decides to bust him. I says, 'You dumb bastard, Nobby. All you've snorted is the ashes of some old woman. All you've put up your nose is bits of her bones, tits and arsehole.'

"Me and the boys laugh and Nobby is turning green and foaming. 'Bits of her tired ol' pussy too,' chirped in Jimmy, and we all goes into hysterics.

"Meanwhile, Nobby, who's bubbling at the mouth and gagging, mutters, 'It's pure horse, Tony,' and passes out. So, I wets me finger and tastes the residue of powder in the vial…

"I couldn't believe it. One hundred per cent pure heroin.

"What an idiot. I'd dumped probably five hundred quids' worth. After that little fiasco I moved on to churches… There's always been a kind of thieves' honour, ever since Jesus' time, not to steal from churches. That was, 'til I come along. My motto is: if it ain't nailed down, I'm gonna steal it – and churches, particularly Roman Catholic, are chock-a-block with gold and silver chalices, crucifixes, goblets, candlesticks, plates…

"I just walked in," Tony smirked, "and lifted the stuff right off the altar. And no big bolt of lightning came down from the ceiling to strike me dead. Far as I'm concerned, God's just a doddery old bloke in the sky who don't scare me none."

Having done over most of the churches within the hearing of Bow bells, Tony and his boys went on a libertine crime spree, robbing post offices, banks and shops all over London.

One night they broke into Fifty Shilling Tailors, an establishment selling cheap off-the-peg suits, and set off the burglar alarm. As they hurriedly piled four hundred suits into the back of a truck, Tony remarked, with typical irony, "Who the fuck would want to waste good money puttin' in an alarm system to protect this lousy clobber?"

Sadly the getaway truck didn't get away. It was out of petrol and everyone got arrested by the cops. Tony went back inside, this time doing a two-year stretch in Wormwood Scrubs, one of the greatest universities for expanding the potential of the criminal mind.

Tony graduated with honours. He returned to the street anxious to pursue a newfound opportunity in the protection racket business. In three years, aided and abetted by vicious thugs, he built a reputation for violence second only to the Kray Brothers. But, unlike the Krays – who collected their protection money from dance halls, strip clubs and restaurants – Tony's genius was to milk the little businessman: the gent with wife and kids, who didn't want any trouble, who ran jellied eel shops; had stalls down Petticoat Lane or Wentworth Street; the betting shop owner; fishmonger; the tailor; the publican; butchers, bakers and candlestick makers. Plus those who tiptoed around the law as well: the hustlers, card sharks, pimps, queens, pushers, and prostitutes…

Every week, Tony's clients forked over a couple of pounds each. All three hundred of them. Six hundred quid a week, which was twice as much as I made in a year working as a boat loader at the London Docks. God forbid if anyone refused to pay or couldn't. For Tony, body parts represented payments that were past due. If you were four pounds in arrears, he'd cut off a little finger. If it was ten pounds you hadn't paid, you'd lose an ear.

"People don't mind losing a little finger," Tony would rhapsodise. "I mean, you can still pick up a pint of beer. But an ear? That's a different story. Lose an ear and everyone you meet for the rest of your life is goin' to say, 'How'd you lose your ear, mate?' And as for girls, forget it. No pretty girl is goin' to go with a one-eared geezer."

Twenty pounds: both ears. Thirty pounds: both ears and a hand. By the time a client got to fifty quid, he'd have no appendages to lop off, so Tony would remove a kneecap.

Without anaesthetic, of course.

People claimed you could hear victims of this unpleasant procedure, screaming from Aldgate all the way to Stratford. Rumour had it Tony collected his victims' body parts and displayed them at home on his dead mother's dressing table, making a grizzly altar to her memory.

One time I went with Tony and his gang to Walthamstow, out in the sticks, to collect from a publican called Louis Fairlough. He was a Geordie and an ex-Army boxing champion. We went in three Ford Zephyrs: two-toned, whitewalls, windows down, arms dangling over the side, smoking Pall Malls as we swigged Ind Coope Pale Ale and whistled at all the birds.

We thought we were the kings of the road.

The pub, The Cauliflower, was one room, a public bar with no fancy private saloon. The place was empty, it being about eleven-thirty in the morning, with the doors only just opened for business. Behind the bar, Fairlough was none too happy to see Tony and eight of his enforcers swagger in.

(I'm not including myself in the eight. I was just an observer.)

An altercation ensued. Threats were hurled across the bar like hot coals. Tony wanted his six quid, which was three weeks of payments past due. Fairlough didn't have the money and said he didn't intend paying a 'greasy Greek Cypriot' like Tony another penny.

Big mistake.

Tony punched him – a looping, right upper-cut that any self-respecting boxing pro should have seen coming. Fairlough, though, was all mouth-and-trousers: out of condition, having indulged in too much beer.

He didn't know what hit him. He rose into the air like a British Aerospace rocket; and just like a British Aerospace rocket, he quickly crashed back down to the ground in a big heap, out cold.

Always the Machiavellian, Tony tied the poor man up, gagged him, and then threw him headfirst down into the cellar, among the foul-smelling beer barrels. Tony then locked the pub door, took up position behind the bar and announced, "Boys, what'll it be? Everything's on the House."

For the next three hours, beer and whisky and gin flowed from tap and spigot. Pork pies, pickled eggs, saveloys, pig trotters, peanuts – they all went throat-wise, in an endless procession. People banged at the door, yelling for the bar to open. Slowly and surely, the gang got paralytic; one by one, we passed out. The ending was a blur. The police came and broke into the place, with lots of, 'Hello, 'ello, 'ello. Wot's this 'ere, then?' as they stood gaping at the post-Bacchanalian scene before them. No charges were filed, though. Allegedly,

Tony had a compromising photo of the Police Chief with a young boy, and so the event served to further embellish the expanding mythology of Tony the Greek.

When Tony cornered me, on Table 9 in the Luciana Billiard Hall at Stratford, he told me he needed a favour and to pack my toothbrush. I was going to Paris for the day, he said, all expenses paid. I should've been delighted and, when he added that I'd earn myself a tenner, I should've been doubly delighted.

But I wasn't.

Tony explained I was to go to Paris on Saturday (just two days away) to meet a one-legged geezer by the name of Bruce at Café Marignan on Rue de Marignan, off the Champs Elysées. He handed me a foldout map of the city. A large 'X' marked the meeting place. Bruce would give me a package, nothing illegal.

"Just bring it back to London and Bob's yer uncle."

Sure Tony, nothing illegal, I thought. And my name's Joe Schmo. But I couldn't refuse. No-one ever refused Tony the Greek, not even old school friends. And besides, I'd grown attached to my kneecaps.

"I'm playing football Saturday. Crucial league game against Dalston," I whined hopefully.

Tony just stared right through me with his dead Mafioso eyes, circulating his cinematic shoulders menacingly.

"Anyway, I don't have a passport," I persisted weakly.

"No problem," said Tony and he snapped his ringed fingers. Jeff the Jerk, his factotum, pulled out a handful of Her Majesty's British passports from inside his Brando-esque leather jacket and handed them to Tony.

"D'you know what I can sell one of these on the black market for?" Tony asked me, waving one of the passports in front of my nose.

I could smell the newness of its plastic cover.

"Fifty quid, that's what," Tony barked. "And, they only cost me a pound a piece. That's an eight thousand per cent profit on my investment."

As I struggled to fathom the arithmetical logic of this statement, Tony rambled on.

"So how does a poor Greek Cypriot immigrant like me become a entrepreneur in passports?" he asked, tapping his forehead knowingly with his finger. "It's in the blood. Us Greeks invented the system of money, economics. It's what Plato spent his whole life in a cave figuring out."

That was news to me. Perhaps Tony was getting confused with Buddha.

"Or was it Homer?" he queried aloud to no-one in particular.

"Didn't he invent homersexuals?" quipped Jeff the Jerk.

No-one laughed (although I thought it was funny) because we were anxious not to give offence to Tony.

"You berk," Tony growled. "The Amazonians invented homos. The Amazonian women were these big, muscular birds – huge. They lived on the island of Lesbos and were always off to war, fighting the Macedonians or Turks, often for as long as a year at a stretch. Their menfolk stayed home keeping the house clean, hoovering and doing the knitting. And, with the wives away for so long, the men started playing with themselves and then with each other, and before long – although it's revolting to think about – they started poking their John Thomases up each others' bumholes."

He paused and grimaced.

"Soon," he continued, "they were all at it and not missing the women one bit. In fact, they was shit-scared their warrior wives would return and discover that they were all pansies. So they all fled to the island of Mykonos, which is still the fag capital of the world. When the women did return from war to Lesbos, and found all the men had scarpered, it wasn't long before they too began kissing and cuddling and doing whatever else dykes do. And, because they lived on the island of Lesbos, they called themselves Lesbians."

Tony grabbed hold of his lapels, schoolmaster fashion, and grinned with pride at his own erudition.

"Now, 'aving educated you bunch of morons on the finer points of 'uman deviation, let me get back to 'ow I saw a business opportunity in passports. See, me and 'Arry the Dip – who's got the lightest fingers in the pickpocket business – used to tour the city pubs on a Friday night. That's when all the snotty suits have got their pay packets and are getting boozed up before getting the train home to the neat little wife. Around seven in the pm, after these spineless gits have had a few gins, me and 'Arry would cruise about eight pubs, movin' through the crowded bars like a dose of salts, with our 'Arry dippin' and then slipping the wallets to me. In no time at all, we'd be sittin' in Dirty Dick's, off Liverpool Street, with maybe thirty or forty wallets, all of 'em nicked in under an hour.

"We'd go through the wallets and find luncheon vouchers, rail tickets, maybe a johnny or two. On average we'd get ten quid a wallet, maybe more, particularly during Christmas at bonus time and then you're looking at maybe a hundred, two even, at a pop. Any old 'ow, got this one wallet, it belonged to a Mr Harold Perkins. In it was an underground season ticket, a paltry pound note, an ex-serviceman's pension card and an official-looking employee's identity card for Her Majesty's Passport Office at Petty France, London. Non-transferable. On it was a mugshot of a sad, scared, old and bald bloke. His address was Sheldon St. Bow. I knew the place – filthy council flats. My Greek blood sensed a real business opportunity with our Mr Perkins. Seemed to me he could use a few bob, if you know what I mean?

CHAPTER ONE

"A few days later, 'bout six in the pm, I'm 'anging about Bow Station. Out comes Harold in his dog-eared suit and worn shoes, hurrying home like a good little mouse after a hard day on the office treadmill. So I steps in front of him and introduces myself, he mumbles something about he didn't want to buy anything, he was late and his wife would worry.

"Poor henpecked bastard, he tries to push past me, so I flash his Passport Office identity card. That got his attention. I talked him into 'aving a quick pint with me at The Anchor. Over a beer, I pumped him to find out what his job was.

"And guess what? My nose for business was, as always, right on target. Harold told me he was a clerk in the stockroom and stamped serial numbers on the front of new passports. So I inquired, tactfully, as to 'ow many un-numbered passports he had in stock any one time. 'Oh,' he tells, 'the Passport Office always has about twenty-five thousand in stock.' Light bulbs went off, didn't they?

"Well, I gave Harold his card back. He was very extremely grateful. Now all I had to do was reel him in and I'd be in the passport business.

"To cut a long story short, the following Friday I meets Harold again at Bow. I don't exactly kidnap him but sort of strong-arm him into me Zephyr and takes him to The Pussy Kat – a strip club used by the motor trade, off the Mile End Road.

"A few gins, a couple o' mandies, and Harold finds himself upstairs in bed with two right ol' tarts and they really gave him a right seeing-to. Meanwhile, I've got Polyfoto Ronny snappin' shots behind the curtain. Mission accomplished.

17

"I later shows Harold the contacts and 'e agrees to… purloin, shall we say, passports in return for cash and mum's-the-word with his wife about his naughty night out.

"Talking of Ronny… 'Ere, Al. Take this passport over to Polyfoto on the Commercial Road. Ask for Ronny, he'll fit you up with a mugshot. Now, you – don't worry about nuffin'," Tony said, turning to me and slapping me on the back.

He swaggered languidly then out of the billiard hall, followed by his gaggle of villains.

As I walked up Commercial Road I wondered, why me? Try as I might, I could think of no good reason why I'd been requisitioned to go to Paris. It certainly wasn't because of my French language skills. At my last school exam, I'd scored just two out of a hundred for French: bottom of the class. The teacher explained to me I could have scored three, but I spelled my surname wrong.

I cursed my luck. Earlier, I'd intended to go to the movies. *The Abominable Snowman* was showing at the Vogue Cinema, a local fleapit. When I got there, all the seats had sold out and so I'd decided to go to the billiard hall. And there, I had my fateful encounter with Tony.

Tony must have phoned ahead. When I got to Polyfoto, Ronny was waiting for me at the front door. He was flushed and agitated, like a bitch on heat.

"You must be Alan," he lisped through thin mean lips, his eyes swivelling all over me. "Come in, dear, come in."

He sat me on a stool in front of a large sheet of paper and proceeded to prance around me, primping and fussing with my hair; viewing my face from different angles; checking his light meter against the shadows cast by cheek and jaw. Frankly, I thought all this fuss was way over the top for a simple passport photo.

"You've got wonderful bone structure. I just know you're not English."

"Russian," I replied, irked at the time being wasted.

"Tartar, like Nijinsky. I knew it the minute you walked in. The English have faces like mutts. Me, I'm Romanian."

Suddenly, Ronny was all business, clapping his hands.

"Okay, Alan," he announced. "Now, we're not shy, are we? You get naked. Put your clothes and shoes in the corner, then come and kneel on the paper, like a sprinter on starting blocks. You'll need to get your pretty bottom up in the air. I'm going to be shooting right up your—"

"What you on about?" I yelled, interrupting his reverie.

"Oh, come on, dear. Don't get difficult. We all need the money."

"Money? Screw you. I'm here for a passport photo."

Ronny's Romanian chin dropped.

"Tony didn't mention anything about a passport photo," he said. "He told me he had a client who wanted some gay porno pics, and you were the model."

"Tony's pulling your leg."

We both laughed.

"Bastard knew I wouldn't stay this late just to do a mugshot. Oh well, whatever King Tony wants."

Ronny gave me the once-over. "Well," he said. "We can't have you looking like a bloody beatnik. Take off the smelly sweater."

He hurried to a dressing room and came back with a white shirt and a camel-coloured blazer. Both were many sizes too big.

"Here, put these on. Did you bring your passport?"

I gave Ronny the passport.

"Where you off to?"

"Paris."

"Rather you than me, dear," Ronny stated emphatically, while he fussed and fluffed my hair.

"Why?" I asked.

Without answering, Ronny swung into action, first with a jumbo-sized hairspray, wielding the aerosol can like some gigantic sword attacking an invisible dragon. Within seconds I was blinded, choking on the chemical fumes with my hair rapidly hardening to the consistency of concrete. Next, Ronny ducked behind the camera perched on a tripod, fiddled briefly with the lens, then shouted, "SAY CHEESE!" I could only mumble a response, because my mouth was glued together by the hair fixative. A flash went off, punctuating my watery vision with a single, bright white full stop.

"Hold it... Smile, sweetie!"

Another flash.

Ronny unloaded the film and waltzed off into the darkroom.

"We've got an hour to kill while the negs develop," Ronny informed me upon his return. "C'mon, I'll buy you a martini."

"A what?"

He puckered his lips in mock surprise. "Oh, we are naive. And queer?"

"No way."

"Oh well, we'll cross that bridge when we come to it."

We hurried out into the wet East End night, where the streets dazzled with liquid reflections of traffic and shop-front neons. The rain was swilling down in endless veils of grey.

We went to The Dudragon Arms. Ronny sipped a martini and complained it was warm; I chugged on a beer. The beer was warm, too: as cloudy as pond water, the glass coloured by some form of filthy brown algae. I knew The Dudragon Arms well, but could never make my mind up as to whether it was a pub pretending to be a music hall, or a music hall pretending to be a pub. The place was ornately Victorian. It had a huge stage and an auditorium, flanked by three long bars that were the watering holes for the four or five hundred working-class punters packing the place every night to see performers strut their stuff: singers; acrobats; strippers; comics; conjurers; and the occasional sword swallower.

Nobody came for the food. It was God-awful. Boiled cabbage, mushy peas, fried onions and greasy bangers, devoid of meat but loaded with fatty pieces of gristle: rubbery, cartilaginous lumps that defied any amount of chewing, but would be used as ammunition to be launched at any artiste who got the thumbs-down from an audience heavily fuelled up on alcohol and speed.

Thursday night there was always Talent Night. I'd entered it, not so long before, along with five other hopefuls looking to win the first (and only) prize of twenty quid. We drew lots: I got number 6, so I'd be on last. After the first two acts, I knew I didn't stand a chance of winning. They were both strippers, with tits like watermelons. I doubted my offering of a poem by Dylan Thomas would evince the same wild applause.

Next up was a blue comic, who machine-gunned dirty jokes for five minutes, and got off-stage reasonably unmauled. Contestant number 4 was an old dosser from the local workhouse, all toothless and gummy. He showered the first few rows with spit, as he sang a plaintive rendition of 'Jesus' Blood Never Failed Me Yet'. He was followed by a friend of mine, Ronny Saint, who fancied himself as a latter-day Elvis, replete with greased quiff, sideburns, and a gold sharkskin suit. He rocked and raved into an electrifying version of 'Jailhouse Rock', closing his act with a leg-scissoring splits that shredded the crotch of his pants and briefly exposed his genitalia, much to the amusement of the few ladies in the audience but royally pissing off the boozed-up menfolk, who became rabid wolves howling their derision.

"Queer! Fag! Pansy!"

Those words and more punctuated their frenzied caterwauling.

Ronny fled.

The next act had to be literally pushed onstage. It was a skiffle group of three pimply lads from Wapping who called themselves The Steel-Driving Men. Despite their macho name, they looked scared shitless. They weren't the only ones. A kind of holy terror gripped me. I was standing backstage, wearing bright blue suede, thigh-high boots (courtesy of the Royal Shakespearean Company's pantomime of *Treasure Island*), tight white jeans, a white blouse-shirt topped with a bejewelled waistcoat (stolen from the wardrobe of a Sadler Wells production of *Scheherazade*). And I was about to read a poem!

I'll be crucified, I thought. No ifs about it, I'm going to have to scarper, run, flee.

Unfortunately, less than thirty seconds into The Steel-Driving Men's plunking, broomstick and tea-chest rendition of Lonnie Donegan's 'Rock Island Line', the audience moved their rowdiness up a few decibels, by banging on the tables with the flats of their hands as they bellowed insults. The skiffle group hastily retreated to the safety of the wings. As one boy passed me, he sarcastically wished me the best of luck, at the same time giving me a look suggesting he knew I was about to be thrown to the lions for the pleasure of approximately four hundred drunken Neros.

There was no turning back. With luck, I'd be jeered off the stage in under ten seconds, which was fine by me.

Ray Martine, a gay comedian who emceed these brutal evenings, was already centre-stage, wildly waving his arms, yelling into the microphone.

"Let's have some hush, PLEASE..."

The noise dipped fractionally.

"Thank you, you ignorant lot. Now, put your hands together – if you can stop playing with yourselves for a minute

– put your hands together and give a big East End welcome to a local lad, Alan Aldridge, who's going to…"

He stopped abruptly and did a double take at the note he was reading from. "Well," he continued. "It sez here, Alan's going to read a poem."

Ray did a coy, pursed lips, eye-rolling, rather-him-than-me look at the audience and sped to the wings, anxious to avoid the first shower of half-chewed beef gristle.

I hurried centre-stage, grabbed the microphone and faced the auditorium. A barbarian howl rose from the audience, followed by a great wave of beery breath and hostility. Out front, there were no faces, no eyes or noses. Just a vast pit of distended mouths howling sonic barbed wire. Panic set the meat on my bones to shivering. Verbal abuse mauled my memory. For what seemed an eternity, I couldn't recall the opening line of the poem. Then, from some dark reptilian recess of the mind, words came to me, not in the right order but good enough to recite, though not in the gentle brown-aled voice of Dylan Thomas that I'd rehearsed so assiduously, listening to him read his poems on a 33 $\frac{1}{3}$ rpm LP. More of a yell…

"Waking alone…"

Some wag hollered, "Yeah, with a candle up yer arse, you little fairy!"

Much laughter.

"In a multitude of loves…"

"Wot's he on about?" quipped a mouth.

"When morning's light. . ."

"Wish it was morning light, mate. I'd be jumpin' up and down on the missus instead of listening to your twaddle!"

A howl drowned out my next line and got louder, and louder, as though the human throat had become a banshee siren. Beer mats started slicing dangerously past me, followed by sausage rolls. A pickled onion blurred by my head, doing sixty miles per hour. Hard-boiled eggs exploded onto the backdrop as I continued the poem, silent as a fish mouthing water. Then, a dollop of mushy peas splattered my crotch.

Someone yelled, "Look, he's peed hisself!" and the whole house orgasmed into a paroxysm of laughter.

There was no point continuing and fortunately the cavalry had arrived. Ray Martine ran onto the stage and grabbed the microphone out of my hand.

"Shame on you, shame on you," he yelled, gesticulating wildly with his arms to quell the din. "You ignorant bunch of morons... Didn't yer mum teach you any manners? Looking at you lot, I don't think you 'ad mothers... Bloody animals. Here's a young man trying to bring a little beauty, some culture into your drab little lives... The only culture you lot know about is what you get in yer bleedin' yogurt."

Ray stopped and smiled.

"Look at all your blank faces," he went on. "You're thick as planks, you don't even know what yogurt is, do you? Anyway, let's end the evening by giving Alan a big hand."

Ray clapped loud and hard, but not the audience. They renewed their howls of disapproval.

Back in the bar, Ronny, on his third martini, wagged a warning finger.

"You watch out," he advised me, spitting the words out. "That Tony is one evil bastard and he ain't got you going to Paris to bring home a French tickler. My bet, it's something to do with drugs. He's into drugs in a big way. Speed, Mandrax, heroin, cocaine, opium... You name it, Tony deals it. Let me tell you what a lowlife scumbag your old school mate Tony really is."

I was going to correct him. Tony was never a friend. I merely enjoyed being a fly on his lavatory wall. I decided not to, and just let Ronny vent. He leaned forward, eyeing the room conspiratorially and whispered to me.

"White slave trade for starters."

I hadn't a clue what that meant so I looked horrified to cover my ignorance. "No!" I said, with mock amazement.

"Yes!" Ronny declared. "He's got pushers all over London: in factories, shops, offices, at dance halls and coffee bars. They sell speed to kids – young girls and boys – and they sell it to 'em cheap. Why cheap?"

I didn't know and Ronny didn't give me time to answer.

"Because it's laced with heroin," he said. "Kids get hooked quicker than you can say Jack Robinson. And, the more they're hooked, the more they buy and the deeper in debt they get to Tony. As George Raft used to say, 'They've got a one-way ticket to Palookaville.'

"Now, Tony puts the frighteners on them: if they don't pay up what they owe, the kids are going to get razored. Sliced ear-to-ear with a cutthroat, maybe lose a nose in the process. Have you seen someone razored by Tony?"

I shook my head.

"When they come out of hospital, their faces look like a patchwork quilt: a hundred, sometimes two hundred stitches needed to hold skin and bone together. Not a pretty sight. Having scared the living daylights out of the poor kids, Tony offers them Hobson's choice: work off the debt by doing a little hooking, as he calls it, go on the game – boy or girl, don't make no difference to Tony, he's got a customer list as long as your arm – and so, they start turning tricks. Before long, he's got them whoring full time. Now, if they're really unlucky, Uncle Tony sends them on a nice holiday to Benidorm in Spain. He tells the kids a bit of sea, sand and sunshine will do them the world of good. Soon as they hit Benidorm, they're kidnapped and taken to Tunisia where they're sold as sex slaves. Oh yeah, there's many a dirty foreigner as will pay a bundle for nice juicy boys and girls. Why am I telling you all this, Mr Alan? Because you can't trust Tony an inch. If I were you, I'd think up a reason not to get on that plane to Paris Saturday morning. And make it good. If Tony finds out you've pulled the wool over his eyes, well…"

Ronny pulled two fingers across his throat and made a gargling sound, suggestive of blood bubbling in his mouth.

"We're getting gloomy," he murmured. "Let's change the subject. Have you heard the latest scuttlebutt on Tony?"

I shook my head, wondering what was coming next.

"Well see, he's in the Bunch of Grapes and he meets up with this pretty kid who's run away from home, up north somewhere. She's desperate to go to the States to meet Elvis, but she don't 'ave enough cash."

"Elvis?"

"Yeah. Elvis. So, Tony – quick off the mark as always – he says, 'What a coincidence. I'm off to the States, New York.

I'm gonna work my passage on a cargo boat from London Docks.'"

"What for?" I asked.

"He suggests he could smuggle her aboard, as a stowaway. He'll sneak her meals and generally take care of her during the four-day Atlantic crossing. Then Tony adds a proviso: of course she's going to have to take care of him, have sex, give him a bit of the other every night in return. She says a prayer to Elvis asking for forgiveness and agrees."

I said nothing, waiting for Ronny to continue after a pause.

"Two nights later, she's smuggled aboard in a wooden crate, lowered into the cargo hold. She's scared, poor girl, but she hears the engines start up and the propellers going through the water. The noise cheers her up because she knows she's on her way to America. Midnight comes; Tony brings her food and water. They have sex and he says he'll be back tomorrow. Next night, he brings two other men with him and explains they're sailors, that they found out what Tony was up to, aiding and abetting a stowaway. They were going to tell the Captain but he convinced them not to, if the girl has sex with them as well."

Ronny kept talking. He told me that the next night it wasn't two men, it was four.

"Tony tells the girl there's only two days left until they dock in New York, and he promises to give her the train fare to Memphis. So the next night, there's eight men."

He went into some detail.

"The girl wakes up after everything that's happened, there's a note pinned to the crate, saying, 'Welcome to America, coast is clear. Love, Tony' and she climbs out, up the stairwell onto the deck, and she screams. She's still in London. She's only been going back and forth across the Thames for four days. Tony was charging those blokes £10 each."

Ronny laughed. The story demonstrated that, for Tony, no crime was off the table – no matter how horrible – not if it meant landing some easy money.

Chapter Two

Friday was half over and there was no enlightenment or divine revelation, no inspiration, no ploy or stratagem or scheme that came along and blessed my fevered brow. This was despite me having rubbed a rabbit's foot for luck and throwing salt over my left shoulder to ward off evil spirits. I bought pegs off a gypsy lady and lit a candle at St Dominic's, praying to God, Jesus, Buddha and a variety of lesser saints including James Dean. I'd had some ideas: walking under a bus (too painful), losing my brand-new fake passport (lame), drinking bleach (potentially fatal), going into hiding (where?), or just admit to Tony I was chicken (unthinkable because he'd kick the living daylights out of me).

One of my ideas did show some promise: use my grandmother Nellie as an excuse. The fact that Nellie was dead was irrelevant. Tony wouldn't know that. The fictional plot was simple: Nellie was on her deathbed. My mum had just got the news by telegram that Nellie had been mugged and so she rushed to Manchester Royal Infirmary – which made it sound factual, I thought. Nellie had requested Mum to come immediately to her bedside, so as to listen to her last will and testament – but my mum was too ill with rheumatoid arthritis (true) and had asked me to go instead.

"Look," I rehearsed. "I'm sorry, Tony. I am. Only, I've got to catch the train to Manchester right away. It's a matter of life and death. I'll shoot to Paris when I get back."

It sounded reasonably plausible. Of course, I'd have to disappear from Bethnal Green over the weekend – maybe catch the Puffin' Billie down to Southend, hang out at The Kursaal, drink beer and eat crab sandwiches by the sea.

As I sat in Victoria Park, though, fine-tuning my fairy tale and readying it for Tony, the plot started to unravel. What-ifs began to worm like maggots through the Gorgonzola of my story, and the mightiest grub of them all was, what if Tony went to my mum to verify my tale?

"Oh dear," my mum would tell him. "Nellie's been dead forty years. That Alan. I'm telling you Tony, he lives in his own little dream world."

Dear God. Tony would give me a sex change with a rusty penknife.

A crow landed on the park bench I was sitting on. It stared balefully at me with evil, coal-black eyes. This was uncanny. The book I had out on loan from Bethnal Green Library and had studied with insatiable curiosity was *British Superstitions* by G.E. Newhall. Only this morning I'd read the entry for crow...

The bringer of wrath.

Perplexed, I shooed the bird away. I saw its visitation as a very bad omen, which panicked me into blind cul-de-sacs of dumb ideas.

Incapacitation seemed a road worth travelling – get sick and be incapable of travel. Gastro-enteritis. A quick dose of the sweats, diarrhoea and vomiting. Go home to bed. Call the doctor, Mum fussing over me with bottles of medicine, Tony comes over, sees me flat on my back shaking with fever. I could fake the vomiting: just buy a tin of vegetable soup, get a mouthful, chew it around, then spew it out. Guaranteed to look authentic. Why not splash some on Tony's blue suede shoes for dramatic effect? The sweats and the shakes I could fake, too.

And then a brilliant idea hit me.

I could tell Tony and my mum I'd eaten lunch at The Ganges. This would elicit immediate sympathy.

The Ganges was an Indian restaurant in Dalston with a notorious reputation for giving its customers bugs in their food that caused dysentery, sickness and fever. About a year before, the restaurant – I use the term loosely – had been closed down for a while by the Ministry of Health. Story had it, a junior anatomist from the Royal College of Veterinary Surgeons ate dinner there. He ordered chicken vindaloo: a fiery stew of chicken in a thick, spicy gravy. While sucking meat from a bone, this bloke noted, with a certain trepidation, that its configuration appeared to be more mammalian than *gallus gallus domesticus*. So he secretes the bone in his waistcoat, anxious to investigate it further in the laboratories at the college. Reaching home, however, he was felled by a virulent dose of Ganges Revenge, which had him sitting on the loo in a stupor for three days. On returning to work, he discovered with horror the bone was from the *genus rattus norvegicus* – the brown rat.

He notified the authorities straight off, and it came to light during the police investigation that the chef was catching these rodents in traps along the banks of the canals oozing through Islington, down to the Thames. The rat meat got used in dishes such as kormas and vindaloos, where it was hidden beneath thick sauces. In court, the chef tried his best to make out that rat was much more nutritious than chicken, and he even claimed it was a staple diet in Bombay. His testimony got him nowhere, nobody was gonna believe it. What he got was six months in Brixton.

I walked from the park to the pub. It was six in the evening. I dumped the gastro-enteritis gambit, as I had also dumped the ideas of flashing at schoolgirls to get arrested and hot-wiring a car to go joy-riding, because at least six months inside was far too high a price to pay to avoid the trip. I sat in the corner of the bar at The Wheatsheaf, surrounded by sepia photographs of long dead pugilists, sucking on a Craven A and swilling its furry nicotine taste down with flat beer.

Paris now seemed inevitable.

Two pints later, alcohol managed to fuel a new possibility. Friday night was dance night at the Lyceum, up west, on the Strand. Lots of hooligans, thugs and villains – including Tony and the gang – went there to jive with the birds, listen to the Ken Mackintosh Orchestra, to drink, but mainly to fight. Gangs from all over London would be there, each with their own turf. Tony's being the toughest, most respected gang, they held court right by the stage. The puny gangs from South London would be way back, near the gents' lavatories, where the stench was unrelenting.

I could catch the Tube to Charing Cross, pay five shillings to get in, have a couple of beers, find Tony, tell him how excited I was about going to Paris – and then head to the loo and pick a fight with one of the South London boys, get purposely beaten up and taken to Charing Cross Hospital. Lots of bandages, put under observation for the night, sympathy from nurses – and miss the flight.

It worked. Except for one detail. I didn't have five shillings to get in. I'd spent my cash on beer and ciggies.

It's a funny thing that, when you need to borrow money, you can never find anyone you know. I went on a circuitous tour of the pubs round Bethnal Green and didn't meet a soul I knew. By ten-thirty, I'd given up the Lyceum idea because the place closed at eleven. So, with the three shillings I had left, I treated myself to a whisky with a beer chaser at the Lord Nelson. I rationalised another idea: why not beat myself up? After the pub closed, I'd go find a house brick and a piece of pipe – anything – and bang my face up, scrape my knuckles on the pavement. Then I'd go lay in the gutter moaning, half-conscious, until found. Next stop, the Emergency Room at Bethnal Green Hospital. I'd tell the police I'd been mugged (a common occurrence on a Friday night in the East End, it's pay night) and could pretend to be discombobulated: dizzy, blind and suffering memory loss. With luck, I could stretch out my hospital stay until Monday.

Perfect.

Thank you, God. I was confident I was off the hook. I spent my last shilling on the fruit machine and, luck be a lady tonight, I won the jackpot. Two pounds' worth of silver shilling pieces poured out into my hand as bells and klaxons announced to everyone in the pub that I was a winner. And only just in time, too, as the landlord yelled at everyone.

"Let's be draining our glasses. Time, Gentlemen, please."

Out on the street I felt quite drunk – but not so drunk as I didn't notice two young 'erberts followed me out. I walked quickly up the Bethnal Green Road, anxious to lose them and put my mugging plan into action, although the irony of the situation gave me cause to chuckle. Here's me, I thought, trying to avoid being mugged by two punks so I can go mug myself.

"Oi, you ponce!" yelled one of my followers. "'old up!"

Trouble. Do I turn and face them, drop Tony the Greek's name and hope they back off? Or do I run?

Under normal circumstances I could outrun just about anyone. Alcohol, though, had turned the sinews of my legs to knitting wool, undermining that possibility. I turned. There was just one bloke walking towards me, a basic skinhead: big overcoat, big boots (all the better for kickin'), and a little rat face with his hair shaved to the skull. Where's the other bastard? Alcohol had slowed my mind too; I should've guessed he was working his way behind me, but I didn't.

"Got a light, moosh?" enquired Rat Face, which was pretty corny, particularly as he didn't sport a cigarette.

He grinned. He'd even got little rat teeth: all yellow, and pointed.

Now's the time to push those horrible little teeth right down his throat. I clenched my fist, readying to throw a punch, when an explosion of light went off in my cranium and pain cranked across my forehead.

I fell to my knees. I knew Rat Face's accomplice had hit me over the head. I wasn't too hurt, just angry I'd fallen for such an old mugger's trick. Now the two skinheads leaned over me, laughing. Rat Face pulled out a switchblade and put it to my throat.

"Give uz yer money, or I'll stick yer."

"Go rob the bleedin' tourists," I spat.

I felt the tip of the blade press deeper into the skin of my Adam's apple.

"Give – or you're a goner, mate," squeaked Rat Face.

While contemplating this offer I vaguely heard a car screech to a halt, doors slamming, followed then by the unmistakable voice of Tony.

"Hey, you bleedin' skinheads, scarper – or I'll have your guts for garters."

I looked up. Tony was accompanied by four of his gorillas and, as they approached, their barn-door bulk was dramatically silhouetted against the car's headlights. The skinheads, burning rubber from their bovver boots, fled towards Aldgate.

"You all right, Al?" asked Tony, lifting me up from the pavement and giving me a big, friendly bear hug.

"Sure, just the usual Friday night close shave with death," I replied, each word larded with facetious inflection.

"Ready for gay Paree?"

"Can't wait," I lied.

"Wanna ride home?" asked Tony.

"No, I'll walk."

"Okay. See you tomorrow night, at the Como Café. There'll be a tenner waiting for you. TTFN!"

Ta-ta for now. Tony and the henchmen squeezed their muscle-bunched torsos, bulging biceps, their ape-like necks, ham-hock fists and currant eyes back into the motor. It sped off, into the funereal gloom.

As I walked home, my schemes all but defeated, I had a mystical experience such as Paul might have had on the road to Damascus. First, a pinpoint of light burned bright against the gloomy backdrop of night. By the second it grew larger until it became a huge penumbrated star that barred my way.

Within the ethereal glow, there stood an angel clothed in clouds. Its face was radiant with sunshine and at its feet were swords of fire. The angel wore a policeman's helmet and in his hand he held a little book open: across the pages was written, *Put your trust in me* and, no sooner had I read those words, the bizarre vision disappeared. Whether it was booze-induced, strain, no sleep, or caused by the adrenaline rush of staring death in the face earlier, I don't know. It seemed an augury from heaven. But what on earth did it mean?

Put your trust in me…

I ran the phrase over and over in my head, looking for enlightenment. Suddenly, the vision was obvious: I had to put my trust in the police. To do that, I had to commit a crime. If I committed a crime right there and then – that night – I'd spend the weekend in jail and wouldn't be going up before the judge until Monday: too late to go to Paris. And what better tale to tell Tony? He'd probably admire my criminal bent. But what crime to commit? Certainly not breaking and entering, the sentence would be a minimum of a month. So it had to be a piddly crime, one I'd get a probationary sentence for as a first offender.

I'd read Jean Genet, and Papillon; anything would be better than doing time in a French jail for drug smuggling.

Almost home, the solution hit me. The high street was deserted. I walked past Cuthbertson the Jeweller and the thought 'smash and grab' jumped into my mind. In the gutter I found a house brick. Throw the brick through the window of the jeweller's, act drunk, then wait for the angels of police and get arrested. I could even stretch the truth, by saying someone threw the brick at me and ran off. After a few moments of reconsideration, I threw the brick as hard as I could, and a great peace came over me. Events beyond my control were underway.

The brick hit the window, which should have fractured into a million shards, setting off an alarm. Instead, to my amazement, it bounced back off the glass and missile'd straight at me, hitting the side of my head. Darkness on darkness followed. I woke up in the gutter, a bump the size of a duck egg on my head. The bells of St Botolph tolled two in the morning.

I'd been unconscious for three hours.

I stood shakily and staggered home, back to Sulken House and its familiar smells of cooking cabbage and burnt milk, urine, fly spray and unwashed dogs, of mothballs, dirty nappies and disinfectant. Of old people dying, toothpaste and stale tobacco smoke.

Back to bed, and Paris by morning light.

Flight BEA 427, a Vickers Viscount powered by four Rolls Royce Dart turbo-prop engines, took off on time at 7:40am from Heathrow Airport. Flight time to Paris: one hour, thirty minutes. The plane was almost empty. I sat in seat 20E, staring out of a large oval window and watching the cliffs of Dover recede between scudding clouds as we headed over the grey English Channel.

If someone had told me I wouldn't be seeing England again for over a year, I'd have laughed. If they told me in less than forty-eight hours I'd be sitting in La Santé Prison in Paris facing a one-year prison sentence, but that in two months I'd be in the South of France – Mougins, to be precise – dining with Picasso, I would've called them mad. If they went on and mentioned that, upon returning to England, I'd win the Edinburgh Festival of Arts gold medal twice; become friends with Lord Snowdon; dine at Kensington Palace; dance with Princess Margaret; paint naked ladies on The David Frost Show; meet and work with The Beatles; be called 'Beardsley in Blue Jeans' by the press; become Art Director of Penguin Books at the age of twenty-two; represent Britain at the European Arts Festival; have a joint show at Tooth Gallery with Francis Bacon; get into a fight with Charlie Chaplin; work for The Stones, The Who, Cream, Dylan; and create a book with The Beatles that would sell six million worldwide, well…

I'd have said they were nuts.

If they then told me I'd go astral-travelling with Jimi Hendrix, and to the strange world of Poptropolis with Elton John, I wouldn't have believed them. Who would? Or that I'd have tea with the Queen and create havoc for Prime

Minister Harold Wilson. Yeah, sure. Like that would've been believable. As for being around The Beatles day-in, day-out at Apple… Er, no, surely not. Write an opera with Benjamin Britten? As if. Design a stage play for Peter Sellers? Who, me? Help create a restaurant called Hard Rock Café? I don't think so…

The list of people I'd go on to meet would've blown anyone's mind. It included Dalí, Magritte, MC Escher, Joe Orton, Keith Richards, Elvis and Colonel Tom Parker… Mick Jagger, Pink Floyd, Eric Clapton, Led Zeppelin… A roll call of rock stars. Mae West, and actors like Richard Burton, Steve McQueen and Michael Douglas… Timothy Leary, Bono, David Hockney and Norman Mailer…

I mean, come on – you'd think that was crazy, wouldn't you? Add Steven Spielberg to the list, you'd be saying someone really had been in contact with ET. But, yes. I really did meet Spielberg.

"I guess fact is stranger than fiction," is what I'd say, if I said anything at all in response to such a future laid out before me, filled with fascinating encounters.

Half an hour into the flight, a stewardess handed me a tray with breakfast on it: an ungenerous carton of orange juice, cornflakes, milk and an apprehensive cheese sandwich, all sweaty and curled. The plastic plate it was served on looked more appetising. Fortunately, I wasn't hungry.

During the night before, panicky as I was with fear, I hadn't slept at all. Every time I closed my eyes, I saw myself as a lamb being led to the slaughter in a bloody abattoir; or, I'd fall into a black void, ending up in a dingy prison cell full of fat hairy men with grabby hands. The fact that I had a raging headache – thanks to the house brick incident – didn't help either. At 3:30am I got out of bed and brewed up the first of five pots of thick, furry tea interspersed with doorsteps of bread and dripping, and Wonderbread toast heaped with baked beans.

I seriously began to regret those beans as the plane lurched over the English Channel. Their chemical interaction with the tea's tannic acid and my own gastric juices had created a combustible gas, which expanded – painfully and relentlessly – in my bowels. Since take-off, I'd been withholding the explosion of this gas by contracting the muscles of my sphincter. But then the captain tannoyed a warning for passengers to remain seated, as the flight was about to experience severe turbulence. The man must have been psychic. Without warning the plane plummeted, dropping about twenty storeys in less than a couple of seconds. Out of the window I saw the churning Channel rushing up to swallow us.

Everyone screamed to God. Me too. I lost control of my clenched buttock muscles and, in that moment of staring death in the face, let loose with a gusher of foul gas that reeked of cesspits and decay.

Next to me, across the aisle, sat a butch old biddy with a shiny flat face, who wore the latest men's fashions from Bucharest. Stoic in the extreme, she hadn't so much as twitched a face muscle when the plane careened out of control. Then the gas assailed her. She let out an involuntary, upper-class, "Oh, my God" and gagged, staring at me accusingly, making curious porky grunts as the smell permeated the cabin.

Other passengers began to stare suspiciously my way. I needed a sanctuary and, despite the plane's bucking bronco ride and the protestation of a stewardess, I staggered rearward, to the toilet, and locked the door behind me. Now I could sit out the rest of the flight – about thirty minutes – and, to quell the mounting apprehension I had about entering France with a fake passport and the possibility of returning to England carrying drugs, I turned to my best friend as a distraction. His name was Marshall.

Marshall was my alter ego; a figment of my imagination. He was a pretend game from early childhood, a make-believe companion. Where the name Marshall came from I can't remember, except it sounded quintessentially English and manly. Like Biggles and Blake, Bond and Bentley.

Marshall was many things. He was a Zen master; a polymath; adept at yogi meditation; a Spitfire fighter-pilot ace. He was an England and Arsenal right-winger and the conqueror of Everest, without oxygen. He was a Tibetan pilgrim, a poet and a polar explorer. He was a world-renowned philologist – breaking the code of the Mayan hieroglyphs at Palenque – and British secret agent. He was an all-round cricketer for Essex and England, an expert on Sanskrit writing, a gourmand and an athlete.

As I sat on the lavatory seat I was back in Gothenburg, watching Marshall in the World Cup – England versus Brazil. The Old World masters against the New, the Apollonic battling the Dionysian, the lion against the panther. Brazil had the lead, one nil, with just three minutes to the final whistle. For the whole match, Marshall – whose reputation (as the maestro of dribble and destroyer of defences) was held in awe by the Brazilian coach Zagalo – had been closely marked by three defenders: Djalma Santos, regarded as the finest left-back in the world; Nilton Santos (no relation); and Zozim. Marshall had tried to use this to England's advantage by hanging back from the attack, acting as a decoy to draw his three markers out of the Brazilian penalty area, giving England's other forwards more space to create attacks of their own, but they'd made no inroads through the vine-like tackling of the mimosa-shirted South Americans.

The English defence mauled the Brazilian forward line of Pelé, Didi and Garrincha, refusing to be intimidated by their silken passing and balletic ball control. In the 59th minute, though, Didi, inside-left, took a pass; and in a sinuous dance, spun past Wright and Clayton as if they were tailor's dummies. He fired a shot possessed of some dark magic; it curved, in an impossible parabola through the air, avoiding the groping fingers of goalkeeper Williams, hitting the back of the net.

With the clock ticking inexorably towards the final whistle, Marshall moved out of position on the wing, towards the centre circle. He was anxious for the ball, and got it: a hard-ground pass from England's captain, Billy Wright. Marshall trapped the ball dead as a doornail, and then turned towards the Brazilian goal in a slow lope. Djalma Santos and Zozim retreated. They knew all about Marshall's ability to entice defenders into committing clumsy, lunging tackles. Time was on their side, so let Marshall make his move... And he did. In a conspiracy between ball and foot, he shuffled straight at Santos and, with a beguiling reptilian sway, leaned so far to his left that it seemed he'd lose balance. Djalma knew this to be a lure for him to tackle, though, and he wasn't going to be fooled; however, the tantalising sway wrong-footed him, just for a moment, enough for Marshall to blur past him on the right side.

Gathering speed, Marshall ran straight at Zozim, who was astounded at how easily his teammate, the great Santos, had been beaten. Now, partly motivated by revenge and anger, Zozim lunged swiftly at the ball, keen to unload the cocky Englishman; but, with a saucy flick, the ball shoots between his legs in a perfect nutmeg – and Marshall dances leisurely past Zozim, leaving him sprawled akimbo on the turf. He sprints towards the closing jaws of the Brazilian defence, strung like fangs across the penalty area. Marshall fakes Pãvo, cuts past him, reaches the 18-yard line, then leans back – readying to lob the ball in a classic English up-and-under – perhaps hoping to find the powerful head of centre-forward Taylor?

Nilton Santos saw the danger and leapt to block the centre – but there was no centre. Like a Houdini, Marshall was gone again. He'd pulled the ball backwards with the sole of his boot and ducked under the airborne Santos, then scuttled towards goal with the panicked goalkeeper, Castilho, crouched on the line, protecting the near post. Marshall saw the referee checking his wristwatch, whistle in mouth, and – with no time left – knew he had to shoot. He swung his right foot back and brought it down in a short, jabbing movement, kicking under the ball. It rose in a high arc towards the Brazilian goal. Castilho, watching the flight of the ball, smiled.

It's going way over the crossbar, he thought. The World Cup is as good as won, and on its way back to Rio.

The ball suddenly dropped like a stone, as the reverse spin so expertly applied by Marshall overcame its forward momentum and dipped, under the bar, and bounced into the back of the net. One hundred thousand throats, mine included, yelled "GOAL!" as the referee blew his whistle for the end of the ninety minutes.

The intercom crackled.

"Would passengers kindly take their seats in preparation for our landing at Orly Airport. Thank you."

Damn. Extra time would have to be played some other day. I hurried from the toilet back to my seat, just in time to see the quaint decrepitude of the Parisian rooftops appear below us.

I disembarked from the plane, down a gangplank onto the tarmac and took my first steps on foreign soil. It was a moment to savour, an occasion to enjoy. This was France, after all. The land of my heroes: Monet, Toulouse-Lautrec, Debussy, Baudelaire, Hugo, Flaubert and Proust.

Instead, I was gripped with fear and foreboding. My heart was banging wildly inside my ribcage, like a frightened bird. I'd read that the Inuit people live only for the now, with no concept of the future. I was wishing I thought like they did. It was the future, thinking about it, that was turning me into a nervous wreck because I didn't know what I was getting myself into.

I entered the terminal and my sense of isolation thickened. Everywhere I looked, the words were incomprehensible –

newspapers, magazines, menus, the arrivals and departure boards, posters – all meaningless. As were the brands they advertised – matelots drinking Admiral? A waiter pouring Cañar? A Gaugin painting of South Sea beauties for Compagnie Oceanic de Produits Coloniaux? A bellboy carrying a huge biscuit, or was it a mattress on his back, for Rita Schaer?

The continual announcements over the loudspeaker could have been in Swahili for all I understood them. In less than five minutes, I'd been reduced to a simpleton. I was gripped with a feeling of utter helplessness. If I could have run back to the plane to demand political asylum, I would have; but, along with the rest of the passengers off the BEA flight, I was being funnelled like a sheep between a double line of grim-faced police towards Immigration.

These cops weren't your rosy-cheeked British Bobbies. They were squat Algerian thugs, dressed in riot gear and toting sub-machine guns. As I shuffled in line, I could feel their eyes staring at me. In my state of increasing paranoia, I imagined they knew I'd entered France illegally; that my fake passport would be discovered and they'd enjoy giving me a good kicking on the way to jail. But why the riot gear? Was something going on in Paris I didn't know about? Maybe an English football club was playing in the European Cup. Frankly, I wished I was home getting ready for my own soccer match over Hackney Marshes.

"*Au suivant!*" barked the Immigration Officer. He was staring straight at me, tiny eyes brimming with hostility.

Oh shit, it's my turn. The next couple of minutes could determine the next year or so of my life, I thought. I hoped the officer was shortsighted. Clutching the passport in my sweaty hand, I stepped forward and placed it firmly on his desk and smiled at him. The officer muttered something totally unintelligible to me. I gave him my best perplexed 'I'm just a dumb Englishman' look. He repeated his command and I shrugged my shoulders. He was getting angry now, his face reddening. He snatched my passport and opened it up to the identification page with my photo. His eyes bounced between me and the picture, studying both intently.

The blood drained from my face and my leg muscles began to twitch uncontrollably. Was I sussed?

He asked me something in French. Totally confused, I twirled my fingers in a circular motion at my temples – the international gesture for 'I don't understand' – and the officer's eyebrows flew up to touch his hairline, while his mouth contorted into a scimitar-shaped snarl. He was really pissed off. Then I realised: I'd given him the wrong international gesture. The sign I'd made was telling him I thought *he* was an idiot.

I quickly shrugged my shoulders and offered up supplication with my open hands, the correct signal for 'I don't understand' and, at the same time, in English I apologised for not being able to speak French. This seemed to placate the angry little man. He pointed to my hair, pursed his lips and did lots of tut-tut-tutting. A glimmer of hope flickered through my mind: maybe long hair was banned in France, and I wouldn't be allowed into the country. That would suit me fine. I'd be back in London by lunchtime, get some fish and chips at Harry's in the Angel, and then go tell Tony that my mission to Paris had failed. I could lie, blame the passport, say it got sussed by the French authorities, that I was lucky I didn't end up in jail – make it sound all heroic-like – and then I'd be off the hook.

But it wasn't to be.

"Your visit, what is the purpose?"

The bastard spoke English perfectly.

"To see the Mona Lisa at the Louvre."

I'd come up with this contingency in London. After all, I looked like an art student: black crew neck sweater, jeans and quirky Yugoslavian climbing boots. What better excuse to visit Paris than to pay homage to the most famous painting in the world?

The officer nodded, even smiled, as he fingered the embossed letters, British Embassy, which Ronny had impressed on my photo.

"How long is your visit to France?"

"I'll fly back to London tonight."

His hand flashed down and red-stamped an entry visa on my passport.

"*Au suivant!*" he yelled, ushering me impatiently towards a sign, Douane, where more uniformed inspectors and police waited.

"*Votre passport,*" demanded a tall officer who looked like Jacques Tati. He smelled of cheap lavender Brilliantine.

Grabbing my passport with a crab-like hand, he stared at the photo, all the while rotating his other hand over his bristly chin.

"*Avez-vous quelque chose à declarer?*"

The declare word I understood. Guessing the question, I told him no.

The officer pointed to my backpack.

"*Pouvez-vous ouvrir votre sac?*"

I unhitched my bag and showed him inside.

"Sandwich for lunch," I informed him, lifting out a paper bag filled with a sweaty Spam sandwich.

He grimaced at the sight of it.

"*Avez-vous d'autres baggages?*"

"No."

"*Merci beaucoup,*" he said, handing me back my passport.

I exited into the main concourse of the airport. Here was the Land of Bedlam. It was as though I'd stepped into a Middle East bazaar, where boisterous crowds swirled to and fro in epileptic animation, with shouts thrown around like hot rivets, while extrovert hands carved intricate patterns in mid-air, or fussed in ornate gestures.

Everywhere was the smell of cooking and coffee, Gauloises and garlic.

I needed a coffee and found a buffet but, like every other eatery in the airport, it was sardined to the gills with rapacious people. They were mauling and shoving each other, desperate to grab at croissants, quiches, tarts, rolls fit to burst with succulent hams, cheeses, pâtés...

There was nothing like an austere English sandwich of thin, white bread with a transparent sliver of meat.

Where's a menu? How much is a coffee?

As I stood figuring out how to make a purchase, other patrons angrily barged me to one side. They struggled to the trough so that they could indulge their delirium for food and slurp oysters, drink bottled beer, chomp cheeses and gobble down wild boar sausages and cornichons.

There was no queue. It was every man for himself.

I saw a clock that read 9:45am. How could that be? The flight landed at 8:25am. I'd spent twenty minutes, maximum, at the airport. Surely it couldn't be much past 8:45am? But another clock confirmed the time was correct. Somehow I've lost an hour, I thought. I'd no idea about time zones; I didn't know that France was one hour ahead of Greenwich Mean Time. Better head to the Champs Elysées *tout de suite*. But how to get there? There were several choices but the Underground offered cheapness, so I followed the Metro signs down an elevator, into the bowels of a white-tiled world of neon brightness.

The walls were decorated with elegant posters and diagrammatic maps of the Metro system, similar to Henry Beck's classic design for London Transport, but the station names seemed so exotic when compared to London's Bow, Wapping, Clapham, Borough and Aldgate. The Metro had Bolívar, Gare de Austerlitz, Garibaldi, Porte d'Orléans, Arts et Metier, Strasbourg Saint-Denis, Croix de Chavaux. These were mercurial names, conjuring exotic palaces and buried cities.

The ticket machine could have been an ancient dolmen carved with Mayan hieroglyphs. It was completely incomprehensible, so I got in line for a ticket booth, behind a group of other foreigners. It was 10:00am. Between these people and the ticket clerk, there were five or more minutes of confused language difficulties. Finally, when it was my turn,

I spoke with great confidence through the hole in the booth's window.

"*Champs Elysées, s'il vous plaît*," I asked, the words rolling off my tongue, loaded with Gallic enunciation.

The sad-faced ticket clerk never looked up from his crossword, nor did he stop puffing on his pipe, which had stained his walrus moustache ginger with nicotine. He punched a button, and a ticket skidded down into a trough in front of me.

I shoved him a nice, clean pound note.

The clerk turned into a clockwork monkey, spitting, sputtering and brandishing his arms about violently. He made obscene gestures with his fingers, too. All the while, his pipe was doing cartwheels around his false teeth. He spat swear words at me; I thought they were swear words. His watery eyes looked as though they were about to pop out of their saggy sockets. He grabbed my pound note, screwed it up with great relish into a ball, and then pitched it through the hole in the window of the booth, hitting me in the eye.

All this commotion attracted the attention of a patrolling gendarme. In a torrent of words and dramatic gestures, the ticket clerk gave the policeman his side of the story, none of which I understood but from the way he ranted, you'd have thought I'd assaulted his daughter.

The gendarme turned his attention to me. "*Papiers!*" he barked.

Here we go again.

I handed him my passport. On seeing it was British, he smiled.

"Are you aware you are in France?" he asked mockingly, raising his eyebrows and putting his face close to mine.

"Yes."

The clock on the ticket office wall read 10:12am. Time was tight.

"France is not a British colony," he hissed, "or part of your crumbling empire."

He waited for an answer.

10:15am. Time was running on.

"Yes," I said, wondering where this was leading.

"Hell itself could not contain worse terrors than the ones we live with here in Paris," the gendarme said. "Creatures lurk in every corner of our city, more dreadful than any that inhabited the primordial jungle. They are faceless men, charged with madness, who would reek havoc with bombs and guns, in an attempt to overthrow our empire of enlightenment, reason, art and science."

10:20am.

He paused to light a cigarillo and took a long, slow pull. He exhaled a great cloud of smoke, straight into my face.

I fidgeted and spluttered. He hid the cigar behind his back.

"Your thoughtless misdemeanour," he continued, "distracts me from my mission to apprehend the malignant wretches who would deign to overthrow our government. Indeed, perhaps your attempt at passing off the lowly British pound to purchase a ticket is itself a distraction, organised by the OAS, enabling one of their bombers to enter the Metro and blow up Orly station.

OAS?

"Hundreds, perhaps thousands, will be mangled, meat from bone. There will be many deaths and all because you, young man, were thoughtless enough to pass British currency in a country that has its own monetary system."

Another long pull at the cigar and he went on.

"I could arrest you for complicity in an act of sabotage – or direct you up the escalator, where you will find a bureau de change. There you can change your dirty English money into pristine franc notes. Go!"

It was 10:30am.

Chapter Three

Ten minutes later I had my ticket. I descended an escalator onto a platform packed with passengers. A train rumbled in. But did it go to Châtelet? I didn't have a choice in the matter. When the doors slid open, there was a lemming-like surge of people that swept me off my feet, and into the carriage. The doors closed and the train rumbled northward towards the heart of Paris.

At Châtelet, I extricated myself from the packed train and stepped into pandemonium. If Orly had been crowded, then Châtelet was doubly so: a solid crush of human cattle, bellowing and grunting, struggling to exit the platform. Spontaneous explosions of violence broke out everywhere, with people screaming and swearing. I joined the mob, shuffling inch by inch like a pigeon-toed geisha, anxious to find Platform 5 and a train to Champs Elysées.

I saw a wall clock. It had no hands. A very bad omen, I thought.

I struggled towards Platform 5, elbowing and clawing, pushing my way through a continuous, oncoming tide of belligerent humanity – only to find the platform was closed, its entrance barred by riot police.

What the hell is going on?

I asked a man next to me, "What is the time, *s'il vous plaît?*"

My French was so obviously bad, he replied in English: 11am. He then explained that a terrorist group – the OAS the gendarme had talked about, which was the Organisation de l'armée secrète – was bent on the destruction of the French

Government and General De Gaulle, and so it had bombe plastiqued the electrified train line near the station.

No trains would run for at least two hours.

"Damn!" I exclaimed. "How can I get to Champs Elysées?"

"Bus," the man replied. "When you exit the station, you'll be on Boulevard de Sébastopol. Turn left on Rue de Rivoli and get a 13…"

The man and his information got lost in the riotous swirl and whirlpool of people. After ten more minutes of subterranean tunnelling, I emerged gratefully into the morning sunshine and the racket of Parisian traffic. Around the Metro entrance was a veritable Barnum and Bailey of beggars – war veterans mostly – in dirty raincoats, and displaying impressive rows of medals.

There were amputees; lepers; a man with scrofula; a sad down-and-out covered in snails who might have been waiting for Godot; and a hunchback tramp on crutches, dressed in tatters, with a huge, elephantine foot. The tramp slid around the entrance, heroically rattling a tin can stuck to an arm amputated at the elbow. I thought God couldn't get much more cruel, but he did. Standing in the gutter was an old dosser, shabbily dressed. In one hand, he held out a battered titfer, the other held a pole, on top of which was nailed a square platform of wood; on top of that, a head sat on a cushion, screaming obscenities at passers-by. At first I thought the head was a puppet, that the hand holding the pole was false, with the real hand hidden inside the puppet's head, controlling the mouth and eyes. Obviously, the dosser was a ventriloquist, throwing his voice into the puppet's mouth. It was good, very good. Original, too.

I stepped closer to admire the puppet's animation and the head spat at me and screamed.

Jesus Christ, the thing is real.

For a moment, my mind dislocated. I was witnessing the impossible. Panic seized me and I just ran.

Rue de Rivoli cheered me up. It was my kind of a *rue*, with rubbish in the gutters, the stink of rotting food and newspaper vendors on street corners. There were cheap shops; charcuteries with trays of *gigots d'agneau; bavarois de crevettes*; tubs of hare terrine and bowls of tripe; trotters, brawn jellies, horse steaks, trussed ducks; aisles of hanging rabbits with their livers dangling from cleavered bellies. It was all very East End. Female shoppers crowded in at a *poissonnerie*, ogling the catch of the day, displayed on blocks of ice: salmon, sliced into steaks; John Dory's; rainbow trout and fleshy whiting; shoals of mackerel and sprat, decorated with exotic marine vegetation; fillets of pike and tragic lobsters, with incessantly active pincers.

On the wall, a mermaid clock. It semaphored 11:15am.

Time to fly.

Buses cruised leisurely up and down the street, but I couldn't find a bus stop. A 136 Arc de Triomphe came chugging along. I ran through traffic and jumped onto the deck at the rear of the bus, only to be immediately confronted by a bellicose ticket conductor.

"*Descendez, descendez!*" he shouted at me, making eccentric shooing gestures for me to get off the bus.

I smiled and offered him a fan of franc notes, hoping to purchase a ticket and stay on board.

"*Non, non, chiens inderdits*," he snarled.

Whatever this meant, it caused a laugh among the passengers. He grabbed me by the arms and, although I knew he didn't intend dancing a tango with me, I was surprised when he physically threw me off the bus. Somewhere a village was short of an idiot.

I fell into the street, with traffic slicing dangerously close on either side of me. Paris, City of Poets? City of Bloody Lunatics, more like. Then, into my comedy of errors, there flew an Angel of Mercy. As I stood and readied myself to negotiate a way through the traffic, back to the sidewalk at Rue du Louvre, a man on a tricycle pulled alongside me.

"*Je peux vous aider?*"

The voice sounded feminine, almost angelic, and conjured images of doves and astrological signs. The speaker was of Pantagrulian dimensions, wide of girth and bulbous-faced, with thick lips that formed a fat smile. His skin was pancaked with a curious, cinnamon-coloured make-up. He was a character straight out of *Alice in Wonderland*, a cross between Tweedledum and the Mad Hatter. He wore a bowler hat, tilted at a rakish angle and, beneath the rim, scraggly dreadlocks sprouted in every direction, like restless eels. An outlandish overcoat of patchwork design swathed what I imagined to be his pale and blubberous body, hairless with alopecia. Clipped to the lapel of his coat was a tiny transistor radio that churned out awful accordion music, while generous pockets overflowed with paintbrushes and newspapers.

The tricycle was extraordinary, too: a pedal-powered rickshaw, decked with plastic flowers and withered African charms. A rabbit's foot dangled from a Victorian headlamp.

He bowed and repeated, "*Je peux vous aider?*"

This man wasn't the sort of character I'd consort with normally but, being already late for my rendezvous with the one-legged Bruce, I had nothing but time to lose. He grinned, and then gestured for me to climb aboard. I did.

"I am Madame Pom Pom, my little sweetie!" he yelled, as soon as I was seated. "Abandon hope, all ye who enter."

He then let out a glorious high-pitched shriek – like Callas on laughing gas – and pumped the pedals.

We headed past the Louvre towards my final destination.

Despite being cumbersome, Madame Pom Pom was an extremely proficient cyclist, pedalling furiously. We careened through traffic with breath-taking élan, carving up cars, jumping stop signals and narrowly avoiding pedestrians. All the while, tinny accordion music was playing, accompanied by Madame's quavering castrato-like voice.

At Avenue du Général Eisenhower, we were forced to slow to a halt as a fleet of paddy wagons klaxoned noisily across the intersection. Nearby, a small explosion shook the street. It was followed immediately by screams, intermingled with the shattering of glass, as a thick plume of smoke fingered the blue sky from behind the Grand Palais. Out of nowhere, hordes of gendarmes arrived, their whistles shrieking as they quickly set up barriers to prevent traffic accessing the Champs Elysées. Horns blared and drivers screamed in anger at the closure, but Madame Pom Pom was undeterred. He swung the tricycle down Avenue Churchill, along the Seine, up Premiere and onto Rue de Marignan.

Almost there.

As we entered the street, I could see the café, just a hundred yards away. We were confronted by a mob of students, or left-wing militants, or soccer hooligans... I wasn't sure just who was rebelling. They stampeded along the pavements, smashing windows, strewing rubbish bins, overturning café tables, yelling taunts and throwing bottles at the bâtonned police, who were in hot pursuit.

The rebels jeered at Madame Pom Pom. One mean-looking bastard punched him on the nose. Madame let out a stultifying, high-octave scream; the next moment, over went the tricycle and I was on the ground, getting kicked and punched. My Cancerian heritage came to the rescue, because I scuttled like a crab between flying boots and jeans, until I reached a deeply recessed doorway and hid, just in time.

The police, baying like animals, their eyes glazed, spittle-mouthed with their blood lust up, jack-booted by, looking to tear a few heads off. As I hunkered down in the doorway's dark shadows, I realised I looked more like a left-wing protester than any left-wing protester there: long hair, baggy sweater, tight jeans and boots. It wouldn't do to bump into a cop. Across the street, Café Marignan was just thirty yards away. I'd give it another five minutes, let things quiet down, then sprint over there to the meeting I'd been dreading for the past forty-eight hours.

Finally, all appeared to have calmed down. As I ventured forward and out to scan the street, a gendarme stepped into the doorway, issuing orders into a walkie-talkie. We bumped into each other and, each of us scared witless, we both let out involuntary aarghs. The cop regained his composure quicker than I did. He gave me a look like that of a buzzard finding prey. He drew his baton.

Christ, he's going to brain me.

I pulled out my passport and held it open at my picture.

"*Je suis anglais*," I pleaded.

He arrested the baton's downswing, grabbing my passport.

"What purpose being you in Paris?" he barked.

Obviously, he hadn't paid too much attention to his English lessons in school. For some stupid reason unknown to me, I wanted to say, "*La plume de ma tante se promène dans le jardin*" – a nonsense phrase that English kids learned at school in French class, but fortunately I didn't. The baton still hovered close to my face, after all.

"I'm visiting the Louvre to view the Mona Lisa," I said.

He pointed at my backpack. "Let me what see."

I handed it over and he opened the bag, gingerly fishing out its only contents – the sweaty Spam sandwich that had festered radically since its last airing at the airport.

"*Merde!*" he yelled, throwing it into the gutter and wiping his fingers on my sweater.

"The Louvre, so how to you get it?" he asked me.

Oh blimey, let's think… I passed it on my way here aboard the tricycle, so it has to be…

"To the left," I ventured.

"*Non, non.* I you escort."

We walked up Marignan together, within five yards of Café Marignan. He stopped at the street corner of Champs Elysées, and pointed to the right.

63

"About ten minute walk," he said. "But careful be, there much is OAS riots."

He stood and watched me as I walked away. After twenty yards, I turned. He was still observing me. Damn. I was going to have to walk round the block. A bank clock unnerved me: it was midday. A commotion, followed by a persistent police whistle behind me, caused me to look back. A gang of youths were attempting to overturn a police car. The gendarme turned his attention away from me, pulled out his baton and ran through the traffic to more exciting prey.

I hurried back to Café Marignan and went inside. The place was all brass, glass and gâteaux. Bruce was at the bar, minus his leg. I approached, and what looked like a maître d' headed straight towards me, making violent Sicilian gestures with his hands, cutting at his throat.

Oh Christ, he's going to throw me out.

Bruce apprehended him with his crutch. "*Un moment. C'est un ami,*" he explained, in exquisite French.

The maître d' retreated, but gave me the kind of look Al Capone must've given Elliot Ness in court in Chicago, when he got sentenced to twenty years for tax evasion.

"You little fucking prick, you're late," snapped Bruce.

Should I give him the encyclopaedic answer of everything that's happened since I left the East End at six this morning? No, I thought. Even with one leg, his broken nose, scarred cheek, cauliflower ear and huge, bony hands sent warning signs not to be cute because Bruce was a hard nut; a real villain.

"And why you dressed like a fuckin' rioter?"

'Ere," he said, before I could answer him. "Take this and stick it up your arse. There's a bog out back."

He had a huge plastic bag in his hand. I was dumbstruck. The bag looked enormous and, never having had the need to put articles up my rectum before, I felt I was the wrong guy for this gig.

"C'mon, get on with it," Bruce snapped. He picked up a small glass jug of olive oil off the bar. "'Ere, take this. Might make things easier. I gotta scarper. Tell Tony—"

I felt a tremendous pressure on my ears as Bruce was lifted off his bar stool and sent flying backwards, into a wall mirror. Shards of glass joined a maelstrom of napkins, wine glasses, flowers, Battenberg slices, all circling me. I was swept off my feet and briefly joined Bruce and the maître d' in mid-air, like we were Chagall lovers.

And then everything went black.

After a nightmare in which I was flying, my arms spread, hour after hour travelling through a thick darkness unlit by stars, I awoke to find myself in a hospital, manacled to a bed, trussed from head to toe in bandages. My whole body was a battlefield of pain; malevolent elves sawed through my nerves, axed at muscles, dervished with jackhammers inside my head.

At the end of the bed sat a bald old dodderer, bookended by gendarmes. He wore a seedy pinstripe suit, its lapels shiny with years of dribbled gravy. He had the furtive eyes of a cold fish and sported a bulbous nose, royally wired with purple veins, and a protruding paunch. Both bore testimony to decades of long, alcoholic lunches. I guessed he was a low-end civil servant.

"Aldridge, my name is Archibald Palethorpe, attaché to the British Consul," he stated earnestly in a toffee-nosed voice, his open mouth revealing dead, grey teeth.

I was right. He was a civil servant. I couldn't help noticing he was holding my passport open at my photo, and that one of the gendarmes had Bruce's metallic crutch, albeit a little bent out of shape. No doubt old Archie was about to bollock me for the fake passport and then he'd have the gendarmes escort me to Orly and put me on a plane back to London, expelled from France in disgrace.

"I have to advise you, Aldridge, you are in serious trouble."

Get real, Archie. Having a fake passport hardly qualifies as serious, I thought.

Archie continued. "I have here a warrant for your arrest," he said, flashing an official-looking document, "issued by the Police Judiciaire of Paris, 7th Arrondissement."

Arron-what? What's he on about? Trust this lot to make a big deal out of nothing.

"I'll read you a summary of the charges," he went on.

Charges? An eel of fear wriggled through my guts.

"That, on August the eighth, you wilfully committed an act of sabotage, placing an explosive device at Café Marignan with intent to cause serious damage to property and persons."

What? My eyebrows almost flew off the top of my head with surprise.

"That you are a member of a banned political organisation known as the OAS, Organisation de l'armée secrète."

"Me?"

He held up my passport.

"You have in your possession a fraudulent British passport. You entered the French Republic illegally, knowing that passport to be fraudulent."

Oh God.

Archie now pulled from his briefcase the black bag Bruce had handed to me at Café Marignan. I had the feeling it didn't contain candy.

"That you transported an illegal narcotic substance," he said, pausing to open the bag and extracting a small, glassine bag filled with white powder. "I.e. heroin," he went on, "into the French Republic."

He took the aluminium crutch from the gendarme and unscrewed its rubber base plug. He extricated a clear plastic bag from the tube, filled with what looked like treacle toffee.

Don't tell me treacle toffee is illegal.

He held the bag close to my face. "And," he continued, "that you attempted to transport an illegal narcotic substance, i.e. opium, to the United Kingdom."

My mouth went drier than the bottom of a birdcage. I tried to tell Archibald he'd got the facts all skew-whiffed, but only a scared and shitless gargle struggled its way up from my throat.

Palethorpe stood, grim-faced.

"If found guilty of these heinous charges, Aldridge – and we have no doubt you will – you'll face a minimum of fifteen years in a French jail. Tomorrow you will be removed from hospital to the La Santé Prison, to await trial."

My mind somersaulted, dislocated, one minute accepting the idea that I was about to be thrown out of France – but now grasping the monstrous notion that I was heading to jail for a very long time. The immensity of this new reality horrified me. Inarticulate, all I could muster in response was some confused gobbledygook. Palethorpe glared at me, turned abruptly and strode purposefully from the room.

No longer the tough guy, I began to cry. The gendarmes snickered, fluttering eyelashes, making feminine kissing gestures with their fat lips. I lay back on the pillow and closed my eyes to shut out the grinning simpletons at the end of the bed, but I couldn't shut out the perverse notion that I might soon be doing a long stretch inside – fifteen or more years. As a diversion I found myself drifting back to the East End, to a local cinema showing *Riot in Cell Block 11*. In the cosy darkness of the auditorium, I was surprised to see myself on the screen instead of Neville Brand, incarcerated and doing solitary, staring morosely out through thick, iron bars. A calendar was superimposed over the scene – one of those big-numbered, tear-off, day-by-day kind. Its leaves were being unravelled by some unseen force and sent careening around me like demented bats, hundreds of them, then thousands, filling my cell. At the same time I watched myself age, from a virile youth to being stooped and grey-whiskered, haggard beyond my years, hollowed-out of life and hope.

This disturbing vision seemed a fitting end to the worst day of my life. It occurred to me that I might have been praying to the wrong deity all these years.

Despite the ringing in my ears, the rages of pain, the raw skin; despite the glaring florescent light that burned through my closed eyelids, and the manacles that prevented me from curling up in my usual foetal sleeping position; and despite the raucous laughter of the guards, I got to sleep – but not through any will of my own. Sometime after midnight, a fat nursing orderly appeared, waving a syringe. I felt its prick of entry into my arm, felt muscle and bone, mind and body turn fluid and flow into a sea of darkness.

In that darkness, ill-lit by guttering candles, at a table covered by a moth-ravaged velvet cloth, I sat opposite an anorexic. She had the necromantic pallor of the tubercular and huge, nocturnal eyes that hankered for moonlight. Her lips, puffy as satin pillows, were painted black as night. Her skin was unearthly, translucent, showing the net of blue veins deep below its surface. She wore a black velvet dress, embroidered with tears of pearls that hung loosely from her starved shoulders. This woman had come to me from the stories of Poe, and I was besotted.

"Wake up, Roast Beef!"

A voice screamed through my delicious dream. I struggled to remain with the vision of my chatelaine, aroused by its erotic possibilities.

"Fe-fi-fo-fum! I smell the blood of an Englishman!"

She shuffled the Tarot with skeletal fingers. The perfumed air overpowered my senses: tuberose, and lilies. She laid three cards before me: *La Morte, La Tour Abolie, La Papesse* – death, dissolution, and wisdom. I was hoping for *L'Amour.* I noticed the card for *La Morte* was smeared with blood.

"Wakey wakey, Sleeping Beauty."

The dream shattered under the assault of the screaming voice, and I spun upwards, through armies of somnambulistic shadows to blink awake.

The sun flared at barred windows. Damn. I was still in hospital.

The room was empty, or so it appeared, until a fat face suddenly loomed into view only inches away, grinning like Alice's Cheshire Cat. I couldn't help noticing the piggy eyes, their pupils so dilated that they had no irises. Fatty must have been dipping into the medical cabinet all night. He turned out to be the night orderly. Readying to go off duty, he was dressed all in white and had a stethoscope around his neck. I was sure he'd given me an injection at midnight to make me sleep.

"Ah, the mad dog of an Englishman awakes," he crooned into the stethoscope like it was a mike. "Someday my prince will come," he sang, his voice swelling to a soprano as he pulled out a pair of scissors from his pocket and gave me a maniacal grin.

This guy was totally out of his box. He pulled off the bed's covering sheet and began cutting away the loose bandages that swathed me from head to toe. Snipping close to my privates, he joked, "Oops, one slip and Mr A will become Miss – and what a beautiful girl you'd make."

I kept quiet – no point in oiling this nutter. Naked, I could see red burns on my legs, arms, and across my chest; the redness was patterned like my sweater.

"Pitric acid ointment," said Fatty, unscrewing a jar.

He massaged the blue medication into my burns, beginning at the feet. He cooed and made little squeals of delight as he slowly and suggestively moved higher. When he arrived at my genitals, he whispered – "We'll save these for later." – and continued upwards, to smear the ointment across my chest and arms. He then got up from the bed and took a bottle and cotton wool from a drawer. He swabbed the raw flesh of my manacled wrists. It was iodine. The pain was crucifying but there was no way I was going to cry out and give this sadistic bastard a giggle.

"I'll be by to see you at midnight with your injection. We can get to know each other a little better," he cooed suggestively. "See you later, Alligator," he mumbled into the stethoscope, Elvis-style, shaking his fat pelvis as he exited the room.

Dumb bastard. Elvis never sang 'Rock Around the Clock', it was Bill Haley.

It was 6:30am. Already it was another bad day.

My handcuffs were removed when breakfast arrived – strong coffee; a baguette; a microscopic piece of mysterious meat; terrine de campagne, redolent of sweaty socks. Everything was delicious, but hardly filling. I was given a grey sackcloth shirt, and pants. A card with the number 74 was pinned to the shirt but the gendarmes never explained why. Under escort, I was taken to a prison van parked in a clingy courtyard behind the hospital.

If ever there was a good time to escape it's now, I thought.

The chain-smoking guards were portly and old, inattentive as they sucked on Gauloises and argued politics. I heard De Gaulle's name mentioned several times, acrimoniously; on each occasion, they would spit gobs of brown liquid onto the cobblestones. Both packed pistols. Beyond the large double gates that closed off the courtyard, I could hear the allure of Paris traffic: the clang of buses, the dodgem squeal of cars and the street cries of newspaper vendors.

I could do a runner right now, I thought. Sprint the twenty yards across the courtyard into the opposite wing of the hospital, then quickly vanish into its maze of wards and corridors to exit onto the streets, free, long before the guards can fumble for their holstered guns...

But I hesitated.

In a perverse way, I was actually enjoying my Parisian adventure; not knowing where its continually changing events were all heading had a certain vicarious allure, an adrenaline, that definitely beat my humdrum existence of working down the London docks six days a week. Now I was rudderless; I had no understandable timetable. I was no longer on the working-class conveyor belt of get up, go to work, come home, go to bed.

Of course, he who hesitates is lost. The guards hoisted me into the jungle gloom of the van, locking me, standing up, into a narrow cage of latticed metal, with no room to even bend my knees. There were ten cages, either side of a central aisle. In the stinking gloom I could only make out bits and pieces of the other prisoners, and what a bunch of villains – like the crew of Blackbeard's pirate ship: cutthroats, thugs, gangsters and murderers, one and all. Some looked as though they'd taken a recent beating, their black eyes and busted lips courtesy of the cops, no doubt.

Through a grilled window I could see the van had come to a halt in a sunless alley behind the assizes, on Quai des Orfèvres. The doors to the van flew open and several gendarmes barrelled in.

"*Politicos, traîtres!*" they roared, smashing their batons on the bars of our cages. Me and the other prisoners were

unceremoniously yanked from the van and immediately set upon by a posse of gorilla-like cops viciously wielding batons. They goaded, prodded, cracked skulls and flayed our ribs and legs. A hefty brick of a fist slammed into my face and, as I staggered, several well-aimed kicks up my arse sent me sprawling.

Bloodied and bewildered, we were herded like cattle into single file, then driven at a stumbling jog down a stairwell into the basement of the assizes, along a subterranean tunnel that stunk of stale urine and carbolic. Then we were thrown into an overcrowded holding cell, where all hell reigned.

Over a hundred people detained for arraignment stood, cheek to jowl, all screaming and hollering, proclaiming their hunger, innocence and guilt. The more the inmates yelled, the more the guards ignored them.

Most of the protests came from the drunks, stumble-bumming all over the cell. There were all sorts, including shoe repairmen bamboozled on Pernod, and blowsy old women done-in on gin. The street bums – and there were many of those – were down-and-out on rum, or cheap wine laced with methylated spirits. Some of them still had their bottles and would furtively swig their grog, then hide it back under their overcoats. Students screamed for revolution, pimps for their lawyers.

The inebriated shared a slurred language. All of these people, without exception, raged against something or other: the moon, their wives, the government, and the price of cigarettes. There was an exception. I saw this one man, drunk into paralysis, standing rooted to the spot, crying as he urinated through his trousers. A voice yelled, "Lord Jesus, save me!" in English. Tramps mooched through the raggedy-arsed crowd, panhandling cigarettes. Whores fought with transvestites.

An epileptic lady rolled around the floor, gurgling foam – and then it occurred to me, based on how fat she was, that she might be giving birth or having a miscarriage. The woman arched her back and, gasping with pain, let out a long despairing bellow. The veins stood out on her neck and forehead, tears rolling down her scarlet face. There seemed no point in appealing for help from the surrounding clowns and idiots, each one involved in their own private verbal frenzy, so I pushed my way through the throng to the front of the cell and shouted through the bars as loud as I could, at the guards.

"*Une femme* needs *aide!*"

Pathetic French, but it worked. I'd caught the attention of a gendarme, African in origin I thought, who flashed me a toothsome smile as he strode towards me.

"*Bougez-vous, bâtard!*" he yelled aggressively in my face. I could smell stale wine on his breath and taste it in his showering spittle. He prodded me in the stomach with his baton, forcing me to retreat from the bars. Disconsolate, I turned and pushed my way back to find the woman but she'd gone, replaced by a pair of young thugs dressed in leather and sitting on top of a prosperous-looking drunk, robbing him of his wallet, cigarettes and watch.

Despite the fact that their victim was screaming blue murder for help, no-one showed even the slightest interest in the incident; certainly not the gang of Corsicans, who were sitting around a fruit box, playing a furious game of dominoes

for cigarettes, slamming the ivories down with incredible force; nor the elderly bag lady, who fished a box of cereal out from one of her numerous paper bags. Immediately, a pair of beggars grabbed the box away from her, and then got into a furious
tug-of-war between themselves, finally tearing the box in half and showering cornflakes all over the filthy floor. Both got down on their hands and knees, and gobbled up the cereal like a pair of dogs.

I circled the cell three times, wasting four hours in the process, though each time the crowd changed as the newly arrested arrived and others got hauled from the cell to go before the court.

I listened above the infernal din for my name to be called out by the guards but it wasn't. I began to worry that perhaps the authorities had forgotten all about me; I found the idea of spending a night in this infernal hellhole really unnerving.

Tired and hungry, I quit my restless perambulations to watch the dominoes game. One of the players, a bristle-chinned Corsican-looking man, stared at me and the number pinned to my shirt and spoke in a language somewhere between French and Swahili, it sounded like.

As ever, I shrugged. "*Je ne comprends pas,*" I said, in stilted, kindergarten French.

"With such lousy French you must be English," he said. "Great nation, the English. Long live the King. Many years ago, kid, before you were born, I escaped from Devil's Island down in French Guyana – that's on the top of South America, arsehole of the world. Built me a raft and sailed to Georgetown, British Guyana. The English Bobbies took care of me like a prince. Under a treaty with France, they were supposed to hand me over to the French penal authority on Devil's Island, but they hated the cruelty of our prison system and let me stay. Best time of my life. So, what you in for, kid?"

"Well, I didn't do nothing," I replied, only to be interrupted before I could explain about being set up for the bomb charge.

"That's right, kid. Everyone in here didn't do nothing. Everyone is innocent of all crimes – but what you didn't do, what the system's got you arrested for, and justice – they are all different things, understand? So what have the authorities nicked you for?"

"Smuggling drugs and—"

"What drugs?"

"Heroin and opium."

"Oh. Jesus Christ."

"Bombing a restaurant."

"Oh, Mary, Mother of God."

"Being a member of something called OAS."

"Throw away the key, English. You're looking at twenty years, if you're lucky."

I didn't have an opportunity to mention the false passport, because a commotion broke out. Two guards were pushing their way through the crowd screaming "*Soixante-quatorze!*", over and over, yanking drunks from the floor to check their pin numbers.

"Hey, English, your number's up," smirked the Corsican, pointing to my pin.

Whatever the guards were yelling meant 74. How was I supposed to know? People were pointing me out to the guards. Things looked ugly. They came and grabbed my arms, and frog-marched me backwards at double time from the cell, upstairs to an interview room. I got sat at a table opposite Palethorpe. The guards stood behind him. As a trio they looked about as happy as angels in Hell.

"Aldridge."

I could tell by the tone of Palethorpe's voice I was in for a bollocking.

"Aldridge," he repeated. "You are a most exasperating fellow. At 10am this morning, your number was called by guards for your arraignment in court. Since then, they have called your number every hour, on the hour, with no response. It's now 4pm. I've been sitting here all day."

What had begun as a quiet sermon ended with Palethorpe yelling at the top of his lungs.

"The court closes at 5pm. If we don't get in front of the judge by then, you will spend tonight in the cells, downstairs. Not a pleasant prospect, I can assure you."

It was a pleasure to be able to respond in English. "Mr Palethorpe, sorry for all the trouble I've caused, but I had no idea *soixante-quatorze* meant 74. See, I don't speak French."

Palethorpe got up. "Let me try and get you in court before 5pm," he said, and hurried out of the room.

Ten minutes later, I was in court, standing in the dock facing a trio of judges, gowned in black, each wearing a small black box on their heads. They reminded me of etchings by Daumier I'd seen in a library book. A prosecutor, dressed appropriately in a blood-coloured gown, faced the judges and read out what I presumed to be the charges against me. Then the prosecutor, looking like a demented Mephistopheles, turned to face me and launched into a violent harangue, accompanied by arm-waving theatrics and finger-pointing.

During this diatribe, I did understand a few words. *Algérie... bombe plastique... criminel... Anglais...*

Guillotine.

The mention of the guillotine flipped my mind from abstract indifference to the proceedings to absolute fear and panic. I noticed the judges' smiles for the first time, at seeing my limbs shaking with terror.

Palethorpe stood and spoke with surprising passion for several minutes, obviously making some kind of appeal on my behalf, then sat down. One of the judges looked imperiously down at me from his lofty dais and gave his ruling in a grave and rancorous voice, then slammed his gavel down viciously.

Palethorpe whispered to me. "Bad news, old boy. Your case has been adjudicated by the tribunal to be political. The French government has the right to hold you in jail indefinitely while they collect evidence against you. This process could take a year or more."

A year or more? That was a twentieth of my life. A year stuck in jail? It was unimaginable.

"I pleaded with the judge that your injuries were such as to necessitate your being returned to the hospital. This was refused. You will be transported to the La Santé Prison forthwith. I'll visit you in a couple of days and bring your court-appointed lawyer."

Two guards gripped my arms and led me from the courtroom. I felt sick to death, drugged and disorientated with fear.

Chapter Four

The drive across Paris to the La Santé Prison, filling in admissions forms at the front desk, the Warden's stern lecture on prison discipline, the nakedness of an ice-cold shower, the medical examination and transportation to a cell, these were all events that dissolved, one into the other, without form or meaning, like hallucinations. It was as if I'd entered the stillness of a muddy ocean, a rudderless boat capsizing and sinking into the Sea of the Absurd. People weaved in and out of my stupor, devoid of substantiality as though they were composed of smoke, until finally I slipped into a bitter and besieged sleep in which there was no rest from the nightmare of my incarceration and the years of imprisonment that stretched forever into the future.

Clackety-clack-clackety-clack. Clackety-clack-clackety-clack.

I was awakened by this persistent and irritating noise. Guards were dragging their batons along the iron bars of the cells. I guessed I was in La Santé Prison, although I didn't remember getting there.

Clackety-clack-clackety-clack.

I sat up. I'd slept on a straw mattress on the floor. The first thing I noticed was the smell, thicker, more pungent than the disgusting cell at the court – an overpowering smell of piss – and then a chemical, bleach or formaldehyde. There was the stink of bodies as well: unwashed flesh and stale sweat.

The cell was tiny, about eight feet square, the walls scored and engraved with graffiti. Names and dates, mostly. There were two double bunks, a latrine and a small hand sink, with seven blokes getting dressed. They saw I was awake and all began talking to me at once, so I had to do my usual "*Je suis anglais, comprends pas*" to shut them up.

Then a blond guy spoke in near-perfect Oxford English.

"Hi, I'm Jean. Welcome to Cell 336."

Three-three-six: an interesting numerological compilation. $3 + 3 + 6 = 12$, $1 + 2 = 3 =$ God the Father, Jesus the Son and the Holy Ghost; past, present and future; birth, life and death; mind, body, spirit; the three magi, symbolising Christ's divinity, majesty and sacrifice; and of course, The Three Stooges: Manny, Mo and Jack.

Life in 336 would be interesting.

The clackety-clack-clackety-clack was now joined by lots of yelling from the screws.

"Breakfast," Jean hurriedly informed me. "We must stand to attention by the door. No talking."

The guards counted our heads, then pushed eight bowls of slop, tin cups of coffee and bread through an opening at the bottom of the bars, into the cell. We picked up our breakfasts and sat eating them on the lower bunk beds.

Jean introduced me to my fellow prisoners. Paul, a pimp, had ten whores working Rue Saint-Denis. He was doing a one-year stretch for living off immoral earnings. Roger, a blackmailer sent down for a handful, he got five years for the attempted extortion of a politician. Albert, a male prostitute, was inside for a cockie (ten years, that is) for knifing a trick. André and Pierre, both thieves, were each looking at a year, having been caught in possession of stolen perfumes. Gabriel, a burglar, he was in for murder, doing life.

And then there was Jean, who introduced himself as a gigolo but was in for assault, a bar fight. He'd been sentenced to half a stretch, which was six months.

Now it was my turn and, with some translating, I related the charges brought against me. Much to my surprise, each charge – the bomb, the opium, the heroin, the false passport – was greeted with wild enthusiasm and accolades.

"*Bravo!*"

"*Magnifique!*"

"*Putain de merde!*"

When I finished, each of the cons hugged me and shook my hand. Albert, who I noticed wore false eyelashes, kissed me on the lips and in a mellifluous, almost feminine voice cooed at me.

"You are indeed a divine angel of the Book of Revelations come to slew the demons of the corrupt French Republic," he purred. "I salute and envy you."

Straight after breakfast came a charming little daily chore. The slop-out. Workable plumbing throughout the Santé was a thing of the distant past, if ever. Each cell had a crapper but no flush. Consequently, by morning it was overflowing with pee and poop; and so, at 7:30am, the designated con for each cell got to empty this bouillabaisse of turds into a bucket. This was done using a tin mug as a pooper-scooper. The latrine bowl was then cleaned and disinfected with an eye-watering mixture of chlorine and ammonia. The con would take the full bucket, while not daring to spill a drop of the offensive sludge because that would be an immediate one day in solitary, down four flights of stone steps to the cellars. There it got emptied down a drain that fed directly into the Paris sewer system.

At 8am the Warden, with several screws in tow, did a perfunctory inspection of the cells, after which there wasn't much else to do but sit on the bunks and talk. The conversations, with Jean translating, meandered from shooting up methadone in Tangiers to how to blow a safe with the new plastic explosives; sadism; sex, of course; and following closely in importance, soccer.

Albert, who had studied classics at Cambridge, suddenly asked me which word was correct: un-navigable or in-navigable?

"Blimey, guv," I told him. "I don't have a clue."

Jean then asked me about Cockney slang. He'd been to London and knew a bird was a woman and wallop was beer. I expanded his knowledge with a few more. Dicky birds were words. Women had other slang words to describe them besides birds, including broads, dolls and scruffs. Having sex could be a bunk up, a screw, a bit of the other, oats and Jolly Roger. Then I explained the derivation of geezer. It was well-worn Cockney for a bloke, a man. Its predecessor was mug, which was derived from tug. Then some bright spark thought a tug was a boat, which it was, and a boat was a steamer. Now, a steamer down the East End meant two things: a promiscuous girl or a geyser that dispensed hot water and gave off steam. So a bloke, a man, then became a geezer because no-one in the East End could spell geyser.

With everyone totally confused I carried on, giving them some criminal lingo. Tickle was stolen money, brasses were prostitutes, lags and cons were convicts and the nick was prison. A peter was a cell, rabbit was talk, darbies were handcuffs.

The slang talk provoked a lot of laughs and ribald comments, to the consternation of one of the screws. He reprimanded us for talking too loud.

"It's not us talking, officer," said Albert. "It's the rabbits."

We all just pissed our pants laughing. Unfortunately, the guard didn't find it funny. Albert got hauled off to solitary for twenty-four hours.

Prompt at midday, the guards did their clackety-clack act up and down the cells. Two men pushed a dilapidated trolley loaded with two huge aluminium vats, while two others slopped what smelled like pea soup into bowls and served them to the inmates. The entourage stopped outside our cell. One of the guards was the dumb wanker who'd put Albert down for solitary. He grinned his simpleton grin through the bars. "Nothing for these queers," he sneered.

The meals on wheels moved on.

"*Bâtard*," muttered Jean. "Bet ya he's gonna shaft us at dinner too."

Jean was right. At six on the dot, the dinner shift entered the landing. Same trolley, same gang of idiots. Even the soup smelled the same. When they halted outside our cell, it was the same dumb bastard screw.

"All you fairies get to eat tonight is each other," he said, smarmy-like.

The dozy android and his factotums shuffled to the next cell.

At seven, all the cell doors were opened. Prisoners filed onto the landing to slowly shuffle, anti-clockwise, around the rectangle of corridors. Smoking was allowed but no talking. Prisoners kept their heads down, not daring to look at each other for fear of the screws, who stood to attention at regular intervals and were slapping their batons into the palm of their hands. They were anxious to bust a few heads before lights-out.

I latched onto Jean, fascinated by his physicality. He was an Adonis. You didn't see many of those strolling about the East End. Even the best-looking louts were beset by acne and bad teeth, flabby bodies and beer bellies; plagued with halitosis, dandruff and crabs. Jean, though, had the physique of Michelangelo's David, his muscles honed and more supple than a snake's. He looked like James Dean, who was my idol, though more gaunt.

After a couple of circuits of the hallways, the screws set up a medical inspection post. It was simply a table, a doctor and numerous bottles of medication. There were pills, potions, salves, purgatives, embrocations and vials, with skull-and-crossbones labels. Prisoners single-filed past the examining doctor. Some got deloused, dusted head to toe with DDT.

"*J'ai la diarrhée*," was a complaint that prompted the doctor to administer a heaped spoonful of bromide powder that left prisoners gagging and choking, desperate to swallow the medication and intimidated by guards, who threatened to aid the medicine down their throats with their batons.

A black man ahead of me stripped off his shirt and bared his back for inspection. The flesh was eaten away by scabs and suppurating sores that gave off an odour of rotting meat. I suspected it was leprosy. The doctor swabbed the ulcerations with raw paraffin. Immediately, the man let out a long

85

agonising scream and a screw smacked him across the chest with his baton.

"Screaming is forbidden."

The black man screamed again, this time from the pain of being hit by the baton. The guard struck him again.

"Screaming is forbidden."

I guessed this scenario could have gone on all night but the guard, aided by a second officer, grabbed hold of the black man and together they dragged him down the corridor to solitary.

"*Petit bébe, petit bébe*," they called him as they went.

My turn. I stood at the inspection table before the doctor. I'd already made up my mind not to mention my burns, hoping to get back to the relative safety of the cell as quickly as possible.

"Name?" barked a guard.

"Aldridge."

"Sir!" screamed the guard, inches from my ear.

"Aldridge, sir."

The doctor ruffled through my hair searching for nits, fleas, and lice.

"Are you a violinist, Aldridge?" queried the doctor.

"No. Sir."

"Then why the long hair?"

Actually I didn't know any violinists, so how the hell was I supposed to know they had long hair? Some prophetic intuition warned me to tread carefully with my answer, as I could be teetering on the edge of a minefield. The only profession I knew of that had a reputation for long hair was an artist; it seemed an interesting route to take – after all, I'd been top of art at school.

"I'm an artist, sir," I barked, confidently.

The doctor nodded approval. "Oils?"

"No, sir. Can't afford oil paint, sir. Watercolours. They're cheaper, sir."

I was working overtime with the 'sirs'.

"A noble pursuit," said the doctor. "Degas, Monet, Cézanne, all great watercolourists. French, of course. Officer Beaumont," he paused, turning to address the guard standing closest to me, "have Aldridge in my office. Ten in the forenoon."

"Yes, sir," barked Beaumont, clicking his heels like some bloody Nazi.

"Any complaints, Aldridge?" inquired the doctor. I could feel Beaumont's eyes boring through me, daring me to respond in the affirmative.

Well, I could mention I hadn't eaten all day, then there were the fleas, bedbugs, the stink of shit, no water to wash with, no bed, plus the fact I was in this hellhole based on a bunch of trumped-up charges.

I decided not to.

"No, sir."

The doctor smiled and turned his attention to the next inmate in line, while I hurried back to 336.

The screws did a head count of the inmates, which took forever. During the whole time – over an hour – we had to stand to attention, no talking, as the arithmetically incompetent guards arrived at different totals, time after time.

When they finally agreed on a figure it was 9pm.

"Lights out!"

The single bulb in the cell dimmed, I lay on the absent Albert's bed. It smelled of sweat with a hint of Old Spice. In the corridors, the night guards patrolled up and down the cells, issuing warnings for talking and whispering, while sniffing for cigarette smoke – a serious offence. They warned against the sin of masturbation as well.

After a while they quit, to retire to their office to read magazines and watch television. A great silence fell over the landing, over eight hundred men locked up and vegetating, only daring to breathe, each opaqued in intimate solitude, dreading the new day and thinking about how to survive it. After an hour of staring at the ceiling, I watched cockroaches in their hundreds emerge from chinks in the walls with their spidery running, doing their crazy zigzagging sorties for food. I hoped they ate bedbugs, because already my body was under siege from their unseen jaws.

"*La Daube de Boeuf Provençale.*"

It was Jean, his whispered voice loaded with sexual musk.

"Take rump beef," he went on, "tender as the buttocks of a young virgin, and unsmoked streaky bacon, pork rinds, onions, carrots, a clove of garlic, orange peel, olive oil and good Provençale red wine, gently boil... As gentle as you would stroke the abundant breasts of your lover... Now, add thyme. Rosemary. Bay leaves and spices. As the sun passes across the sky, hour after hour under fire's magical caress, the meat is transformed. It becomes tender, as tender as the silky flesh of a woman's most secret place... Tender enough to cut with a spoon."

I could hear the salivations of my cellmates.

"Add a *persillade* of finely chopped garlic, parsley, an anchovy, sprinkle in a few capers and black olives... Serve at the last rays of sunlight, when fireflies rise from the fields to dance."

"You bastard, Jean," whispered Roger the blackmailer, smacking his lips. "I was, 'ow Alan say, slipping a length to Brigitte Bardot, when—"

Without warning, a screw loomed at the cell door.

"If I hear so much as a belch from you fairies, I'll have you all in solitary, *comprenez-vous?*"

No-one answered.

The silence, the darkness, slowly enveloped my senses. I dozed off into a fitful sleep, weaving in and out of half-dreams, waking wide-eyed, then crashing back down into blackness until...

Clackety-clack-clackety-clack. Clackety-clack-clackety-clack.

Time to get up and face a new day in Hell.

After breakfast and slopping out, I was manacled and escorted by guards down endless stairs into the deepest bowels of the prison, to what looked like a dungeon now converted into a washhouse. Its granite walls were painted blood red, inscribed with graffiti and pornographic hieroglyphs. There were twenty showerheads along one wall but no on/off controls, each numbered and partitioned. The floors were greasy with soap scum and swathes of thick black dirt mixed with hair.

I dreaded to imagine how many voracious little verruca viruses lay in wait, ready to gnaw into my bare feet.

One of the guards, who reminded me of Anthony Quinn – he had the same busted-up mug – unlocked my bracelets, and then ordered me to strip and stand to attention. Naked, I waited like some dumb animal for the next order. After the fetid air of the cell, the washroom was positively arctic. I began to shiver, violently. The guards thought this was very funny and laughed. They made what I assumed were disparaging remarks, with lewd gestures as they lit up their cigarettes.

"*Quinze*," barked the Anthony Quinn look-a-like, pointing to the showers.

Again, because of the linguistic obstacles French presented to me, the order was incomprehensible. I skated slowly across the slick floor, to the line of showerheads – but then I dithered, because there were no valves to turn on the water.

"*Quinze!*" screamed the second guard, a lamppost of a man, grey-haired and emaciated.

Suddenly, shower number fifteen showed signs of activity, dribbling a few pathetic drops of water every few seconds.

"*Quinze!*" yelled both guards in unison.

I stood beneath the trickle and the freezing water rivuleted down my body, stinging my sore skin. There was no soap, so I scrubbed my flesh with my hands, attempting not only to get clean but to keep warm. When I bent to wash my legs I let out an involuntary scream. They were covered in fleas. Oh Christ, I hated fleas. I grew up with fleas. In the summer, the tenements of the East End got overrun with these cunning bloodsuckers. Us kids were eaten alive on a nightly basis, with no medications or salves to ward the blighters off. They were impossible to catch, too, having a built-in early warning system that alerted the creatures of changes in air pressure, such as caused by an approaching hand. They would spring away with an almighty leap, to hide in a carpet or curtain and then return, under cover of darkness, to satiate their blood lust.

How sublimely God had designed the flea, for when you finally caught one of the little bastards and squeezed it gleefully between thumb and forefinger, with every ounce of strength you possessed, and then opened your hand, anxious to view its crusty corpse all squashed and bloodied, you'd be amazed. The flea would nonchalantly spring away, unhurt. You couldn't believe how this minute creature could withstand such enormous crushing pressure.

Then, in the school library, I found a huge etching of a flea reproduced in a book, *Micrografia*, by the naturalist Robert Hooke and published in 1708. Hooke had viewed the flea through a microscope and then drew the critter in magnificent detail, twenty inches wide (a magnification of x520). I was both horrified and fascinated by the elegance of its design. The flea was a perfect blood-sucking machine, its flat body able to withstand compression up to a thousand times its body weight and yet it could inflate to twenty times its volume when gorged with blood. The ridiculously large and kangaroo-ish legs were adapted for jumping, the saw-toothed proboscis for cutting skin. The hairs, which acted as its early warning radar system, they were what detected the changes in air pressure. And let's not forget it was the lowly flea, carrier of the bubonic plague, which swept across Europe like a scythe. The Black Death killed forty-three million people and now the fleas were all over me.

I was freaking out.

The lamppost-looking guard yelled at me to get dressed. I ignored him and carried on frantically searching my armpits and pubis for fleas. Call it pediculophobia (fear of being lousy, that is), but I couldn't stomach the idea of having those blood-sucking parasites living on me. Next thing, the room spun upside down, as a punch connected with the side of my head. I was on my back staring up at Anthony Quinn's delirious eyes, charged with violence. I quickly curled up in a desperate position of defence, knees pressed against my forehead, elbows tight at my side, as kicks and punches jolted into bones up and down the length of my body. I was lifted up by a baton chokehold around my throat, and then carried up claustrophobic stairwells at great speed.

Before I had a chance to comprehend what was happening, I got thrown into a cell, along with my shirt and pants. The iron door clanged shut. A bolt slid noisily into place. I ached all over. I was alone in a coffin-sized chamber, obviously solitary. I had a feeling I wouldn't be seeing the doctor at ten. The cell measured six feet by three. An iron bedframe covered by a filthy mattress hung by chains from the stone wall. A bright light shone from the ceiling, the bulb guarded by a metal grill. The door had a tiny spyhole for guards to watch inmates. For hours I sat, obsessed with methodically searching my clothes and body, extricating fleas; however, trying to kill them, as always, proved an interesting exercise in frustration – until I discovered the single most effective way of dispatching them: eat the pesky bastards.

After squeamishly cracking the first two or three between my teeth, just knowing they'd been dispatched to Flea Hell forever – and couldn't be returning to feed off me – encouraged me to nosh them down with a vengeance. By early afternoon, there were no more to be found.

Far away I heard the clatter of a trolley and figured it must be dinnertime. An hour went by where I sat, anxiously hoping to hear the bolt slide open with the arrival of food, but it didn't. When I heard the guards calling for lights out, I gave up hope.

I did my twenty-four hours in solitary. The light burned bright the whole time, making sleep difficult. The threadbare mattress was the headquarters for battalions of bedbugs armed to the teeth. Screws were grinding open the peephole hourly, yelling at me.

"*Couchez-vous!*"

Sleep became impossible. Finally, when I dozed off around three in the morning, a guard clanked open the cell door immediately to give me a tray of dry bread and foul-smelling water. This was part of some psychological game plan, to make solitary an unforgettable experience.

When I got out I'd missed lunch.

Back at 336, my penance continued. The cell was on strict silence, no meals. Albert and Roger had got into a fight over smokes. The screws searched the cell, turning up a blade hidden behind an air vent. Until someone confessed to owning the shiv, the silence rule was in force. So we sat on bunks, not daring to look at each other for fear of sniggering. Outside, a guard stood, waiting to escort the confessor to solitary.

Dinner of beef stew clattered by without stopping at Cell 336. It smelled good. With just a crust of bread and a few fleas to eat during the past forty-eight hours, I thought pigswill would've smelled and probably tasted good, too.

At lights out, our cell remained lit. We had to stand to attention in silence. As the night guards patrolled past our cell they hissed at us.

"Cowards!"

We all nervously glanced between ourselves, hoping to see one face betray its guilt, all anxious for the ordeal to end. Time moved in slow motion. I felt dizzy with hunger, ready to pass out, when the Warden – a gorilla in uniform – accompanied by two guards, unlocked the cell and entered.

The Warden made a short but not sweet speech.

"Taking responsibility for your actions is essential under our penal system if you are to become worthy citizens of France and not repeat offenders," he informed us. "It is 10pm. At 10:01pm exactly, if no-one has confessed to ownership of the knife, all five of you will get one hundred and eighty days in solitary."

He looked intently at his watch. The clock was ticking. I felt like being sick but my stomach was empty. All I could manage was to retch, violently.

"Half a minute gone," barked the Warden.

I counted the seconds off in my mind... 25... 24... 23...

In a moment of blind panic, I thought of volunteering to be guilty but fortunately my tongue, brain and vocal chords were out of sync with my fear. I only managed a whimpered gargle.

"*Dix... neuf... huit...*" rasped the Warden. "*Sept... six... cinq...*"

I felt doomed. Having done one day in solitary, I knew I couldn't go a hundred and eighty days with just bread and water.

"*Quatre... trois...*"

Robert stepped forward. "The knife is mine," he said, in a nonchalant manner.

Christ, that was close.

The guards instantly manhandled him from the cell, threw him against the wall, then dragged him feet-first to solitary, followed by the brutish Warden.

Our cell light went out. We lay in silence, emptied of talk, each of us thankful to still be in Cell 336. As I was falling asleep, a long harrowing scream, high-pitched – like a dog being eaten alive by coyotes – tore through the silence, and then another. That second scream continued for about a minute, then spiralled down to nothing more than a whimper.

"Bastards just hot-wired Robert's dick," whispered Jean angrily.

Sleep brought me nightmares.

Clackety-clack-clackety-clack. Clackety-clack-clackety-clack. After breakfast, after slop-out, guards escorted me to the doctor's office. It was a room of learning: leather-bound books, anatomical charts, the musk of medicines and formaldehyde. Through a barred window I could see the rooftops of Paris, burnished with summer sunshine. I heard street traffic and a barrel organ playing.

"Ah. Aldridge the violinist," quipped the doctor as I entered.

"Artist, sir."

"Watercolourist, I believe."

"Yes, sir. And, as befits my profession, starving. Sir."

The doctor smiled. "I'm Doctor Albert Etienne, Aldridge," he said, offering me his hand.

Before grasping the proffered hand, I glanced nervously at my bear-shouldered guard, not wanting his baton bouncing on the back of my skull for being out of order.

The guard remained granite-faced, so I hesitated.

"It's okay, Aldridge," insisted the doctor, leaning further across the desk.

So we shook hands.

"Aldridge, here's a photo of my wife," he said, handing me a postcard-sized print. "Would you make a watercolour copy, say, twice as big? It will be my birthday present to her."

Painting portraits was something I'd never done, but it offered me an opportunity to escape the tedium of the daily routine.

"I'll do my best, sir."

The doctor handed me a well-worn palette of watercolours containing twelve smudgy discs of primary colours, several tired paintbrushes, a 2B Caran d'Ache pencil and a couple of sheets of heavy paper.

"I'll need the painting this time tomorrow," he said. "So I can get it framed." He turned away for a moment. "Guard, tell Warden that Aldridge is allowed to paint in his cell."

"Sir," snapped the guard, eyeing me with hostility.

Back in the cell I got seated on a bunk, set up the photo and, with pencil in hand, began the tentative process of sketching the woman's face. At first I was stroking wispy lines and faint curlicues on the dimpled paper, until – in an unexplainable process – the form of the woman took shape.

Jean, André, Pierre, Paul and a new prisoner, Tali Bahwani – a black man from Algeria doing life for murder – postured silently behind me. As eyes or lips took shape out of the thickets and tangle of lines, they would let out tiny gasps of admiration or whisper words of flattery. Slowly and surely, the pencil stroked and caressed its marks upon the paper as my eye interpreted the nuances of shape and shadow in the photo.

The drawing became a meditation, one that absorbed me totally. I became unaware of my surroundings – the prison, the prisoners, their stench of humanity. Instead, it was the drawing that came to life. I could feel the woman's pain and sensuality, smell her talcum powder, the hint of her lavender eau de toilette. Finally I painted over the pencilled outline with transparent washes of colour on colour – wavy ribbons of brown; splashes of red; dusky greys and daubs of yellow.

When I thought it was done, it was done.

After a dinner of some kind of animal minced with gravy, followed by acorn coffee and the nightly half-hour shuffle around the caged landing, we retired to the cell for the evening. We lit up Gauloises, and relaxed.

André the tealeaf was the first to vent off.

"Damn screws," he growled. "Those bastards are gonna kill Robert. He'll never last one hundred and eighty days.

Those scum are either ex-Foreign Legion or Corps Républicain de Sécurité, and they know how to torture a guy. You heard Robert screaming? They've got electrodes to his ears, fingers, cock and testicles. Zap on two hundred and fifty volts, watch his skin burn black, the brain fry as the heart races to a hundred and fifty beats a minute, and then you pass out. And, when you wake up, they do it again. Poor bastard."

"So Tali, who'd'ya kill?" Jean asked our new cellmate.

Tali looked like a huge piece of ebony furniture: strong and immobile. But, at Jean's question, he swelled up like a bladder and grew enormous, sighing with indignation. He gyrated his eyes nervously around the night of his face.

"I'm innocent."

We all laughed and Tali's mouth split open in a half-mile smile of pearly Colgates.

"I'm cruisin' Saint-Lazare Station," said Tali in a rich, deep bass voice that conjured up images of Africa. "I was looking for marks to roll. I goes to the bar there. I think it's called Bar Locomotive. I sees this guy, obviously queer, obviously drunk, with a wallet fatter than a pig at Christmas. I buys him a drink, he buys me one. I'm workin' against time because he's got a train to catch to Le Havre, spending the weekend with his wife and kids. So, I strokes his arse and suggests we cruise to the pissoire. In a stall I get him to drop his pants, then kneel down in front of him, he strokes my head – and I grab his ankles and yank them upward. The guy crashes into the wall, then down to the floor. I'm on 'im in a flash, knife at his throat, liftin' that wallet right out of his jacket pocket. I'm already dreamin' 'bout the junk it's gonna buy but the bozo makes a violent grab at me, an' me knife sinks deep into his throat. The stupid bastard is thrashing around on the blade like a fish, blood spurtin' everywhere, so I get the fuck out of the stall. The guy's trying to scream but only gurgles because of all the blood in his mouth. Christ, it was a nightmare, man, men pissin' seeing me do a runner out of the loo. I knew I was cooked. The wallet had thirty thousand francs. I bought me some shit, checked into a cheap hotel, shoots up and lurch off to fairyland... When I wake I'm in prison, facing a murder rap. So what's your game, pretty boy?"

Jean smiled. "Nothing so dangerous or uneducated as you, Tali. I simply escort wealthy ladies to charity balls and cocktail parties. I get well rewarded for my services."

"You're some kind of stud to old dames?"

"He's a gigolo," quipped Pierre.

An Arab man appeared outside our cell dispensing fresh water. We all got half a mug.

"Any kif?" said Tali. "Better still, heroin?"

"Kif, heroin, anything. Kif, ten cigarettes. Heroin, 1/2 gram with clean needle, twenty-five cigarettes," responded the Arab.

"I'll think about it," said Tali, turning back to Jean. "So, what does a gigolo do?"

"As little as possible," smirked Jean. "I work the fancy hotels, George V, Ritz in Paris, The Carlton in Cannes, enjoying the company of rich and lonely women. They pay me well for the time I spend with them."

"Do they pay by the inch or the hour?" queried Tali, and we all laughed.

A guard yelled "Lights out!" and the cell went dark. Silence was in force as we all scrambled into our bunks, anxious to continue the conversation but not daring to.

I awoke sometime in the middle of the night to the sound of groaning. Blinking, I saw the Arab was leaning through the bars and masturbating Pierre. I learned later that Pierre was Jewish and his religion forbade him from touching or handling himself in any sexual way, so he paid someone else to do his dirty work.

I fell back to sleep.

Chapter Five

Clackety-clack-clackety-clack. Clackety-clack-clackety-clack.

After slop-out, the Warden came to the cell to collect the painting for the doctor. He was angry, although I had no idea why. He yelled threats at me in broken English, scowled at me, spat in my face. He threw his arms all over the place, in operatic gestures. For a minute, I thought he was going to tear the portrait up as he slapped it with the back of his hand, making puking sounds in between insults. He rammed his huge fist into my chest instead, sending me crashing to the floor as he stormed out.

Jean helped me to stand and quickly explained the situation. "The Warden is pissed at you, Alan. The doctor ordered him to let you paint in the cell. At first, the Warden refused to allow it but the doctor threatened to go to the governor of the prison, so he acquiesced but took it as a personal affront to his power. He's ordered you down to the kitchens to work as a *plongeur* – a dishwasher."

Funnily enough, it hadn't occurred to me that La Santé had a kitchen. It was almost laughable to think that anyone spent any time preparing our meals; they were so diabolically awful.

A screw escorted me down a winding ill-lit staircase. After just a few steps, a fierce and stenching breath rose from below, fetid and suffocating. It smelled of rancid fat and dirty laundry. The temperature swelled into the hundreds. Dreadful noises, absolutely unearthly noises, caterwauled from the belly of the stairwell: the din of crashing metal, loud obscenities and a fearful roaring of furnaces. I hesitated on the steps, imagining obscure monsters of every shape lying in wait – but the guard's baton jabbed in my ribs, encouraging me further downward into the nightmarish gloom.

The stairwell tightened into a low tunnel, its walls slimed with leprous growths, festooned with steam pipes of every diameter, some finger thin, others thick as pythons, all hissing and gurgling like blood in a busted windpipe. The tunnel opened onto a kitchen that looked like a torture chamber of the Inquisition; a low-arched dungeon, murky with steam and smoke, the floor covered by layers of stagnant filth runnelled with oozy liquids.

Flame flowered beneath vats or on stovetops, hellish fires in the subterranean darkness. Through the miasma, wraiths flitted, half-naked in bloodied aprons, their fat greasy bodies drenched in sweat, yelling incomprehensible orders, bumping into each other, cursing, all mad-eyed. They staggered around with bowls of bloody organs or slabs of flesh, as if in a delirium.

Out of the smoke and fire stepped a huge beast, vast and round in the body, thick-necked, low-browed, hairy as a gorilla and dragging a clubfoot. A barbaric figure, clenching a meat carver in one hand and the hindquarters of a horse in the other, all the time his tiny head rolling this way and that on top of his thick neck, screaming orders. I guessed him to be the head chef of this madhouse.

The screw spoke to the gorilla, and they each stared at me with hostile intent. The conversation ended with both of them laughing uproariously. Fear iced through me. I knew the beast was going to be cruel, tyrannical.

He will be bestial. I know he'll hurt me. I'm scared.

Gorilla's demented eyes stared unblinking at me for a full five minutes. If he was trying to unnerve me, he was succeeding royally. I dreaded to think what madness was being conjured up inside his primordial brain. Finally, he points to an oven with his carver and growls words at me in an accent that sounded closer to Russian than French. I stood rooted to the spot and hesitantly shrugged my shoulders.

"*Je suis Angleterre,*" I stammered pathetically.

"Ollier!" shouted the gorilla over the kitchen's noise and quarrelling. A small, utterly spineless man with dead-white skin, wearing only a grease-stiffened apron, shuffled out of the swirl of steam and stood hang-dogged and servile in front of the beast. They spoke briefly, then the gorilla hurried away into the gloom, dragging the horse haunch behind him through the ever-thickening compost of trampled food.

"Duc El Baraka wants you to clean the baking oven," whined Spineless, in English. Every word began and ended with a pronounced click from his loose false teeth. "Clean as a new pin, inside and out." He handed me a filthy cloth. "Use this and plenty of elbow grease. You will get bread and water when you have finished. Not before."

The oven was made of cast iron, built at the turn of the century. There were six gas rings on the range and a huge cooking space, wide and deep enough to roast a complete cow. From top to bottom, inside and out, the oven had a thick gooey coating of black grease, which bubbled and pulsated under the tropical heat of the kitchen. I stood for no more than thirty seconds evaluating how and where I'd begin the cleaning process, when Chef Duc El Baraka lumbered threateningly towards me, already screaming and cursing louder than a pack of banshees. He no longer had the horse leg but instead he was gripping a handful of bloody liver.

Dotted among the gobbledygook he was yelling, I heard the word fay mentioned, many times. From my readings of Shakespeare, specifically *A Midsummer Night's Dream*, I knew *fay* was French for fairy; that, combined with the fact that the gorilla was now spinning around me like a demented ballerina, pirouetting on tippy toes, I figured he was calling me a fairy. As in, queer. This didn't bother me. I was much more concerned about the liver.

The gorilla grabbed me by the wrists, holding them in a blood-stopping grip with his livered-up hands. He then vigorously shook my arms up and down, in what I guessed was an approximation of a cleaning action. At the same time he was yelling at me.

"*Allez! Allez! Allez!*"

He was inches from my eardrum. I got the message and then he performed an act that was truly bizarre. He stood glowering at me, posturing like a Sumo wrestler, and began smearing his hairy arms with the liver until they were matted with blood. This reminded me of tribes ritually painting their bodies with blood before going into battle. Was I to interpret Gorilla's behaviour as his declaration of war on me? Whatever it meant, it scared the living daylights out of me. With an enthusiasm for elbow grease, I began vigorously cleaning the oven. Gorilla watched me, smiled approvingly, patted me on the head, and then ambled off.

The outside of the oven took more than five hours of intense physical effort to get clean. Occasionally, Ollier would stand mournfully watching my progress, then hurry away to report to the gorilla. Several times I asked him if I could have a cup of water; on each occasion, he'd shuffle off to talk to the gorilla but return empty-handed, shrugging his shoulders. "It's not possible," he meekly told me.

"It's not possible," he meekly told me.

After all those hours of enduring 120°F (49°C) heat, I was fainting with thirst.

Screw this, I thought. I'm getting myself a drink.

I pushed my way through the frantic activities of the kitchen hands to a sink. I found a cup, filled it with water and lifted it thirstily to my lips.

A huge, hairy hand blurred into view, swiping the cup and sending it bouncing into the carpet of rubbish. I didn't need to look to know it was the gorilla. I was in trouble. He went off his rocker, shouting fit to burst his lungs. He went on and on, until his face went through every hue from red to deep purple.

When he stopped, Ollier chirped up.

"You are here to work, not eat and drink. When you have finished the oven cleaning, you will be given bread and water, not until. The Duc El Baraka will tolerate no further infraction of this rule. To do so would be to risk death by aspic."

Confused, I returned to the oven where I still had to clean the inside. Like the outside, the inside had years of accumulated crud, not soft and gooey but a thick and hard crust, baked black. I reckoned it'd take me until well past midnight to elbow grease it away, until I purloined a metal spatula and a peeling knife. I began hacking and chipping. In no time at all, I'd scraped the door down to its original metal.

Cleaning the inside of the oven presented a serious problem I hadn't counted on, though: my deep-rooted claustrophobia. When I put my head into the confines of the oven, within a minute an overwhelming sense of panic and suffocation assailed me, forcing me to quickly withdraw, shaking with fear.

The fear went back to when I was a kid. Whenever I was a naughty boy, my mum would lock me in a tiny cupboard under the stairs. Inside was pitch black and coffin-sized. Scared of the dark and the malignant little dwarves who lived in the cupboard according to my mum, creatures that loved to eat up bad little boys, I'd shout out.

"Mummy, I'll be a good boy. Let me out. Mummy, I'll be a good boy. Let me out!"

I'd often remain in the cupboard for over an hour, my horror of dark confined spaces ballooning.

For two hours, though, I stoically faced my fears, working like a miner, chipping away at the oven walls. I found that, if I clenched my eyes shut and imagined I was in a cathedral working as a stonemason, the claustrophobia abated. After those hours had gone by, I had only the end wall of the oven left to clean, but this meant literally crawling into the oven, lying on my stomach to work. As I stood plucking up courage and holding down a feeling of dread, of being swallowed by the oven, that knotted my guts and caused me to dry retch, the gorilla put in an appearance. Ollier was sniggering at his rear.

Gorilla nodded his pleasure as he surveyed the exterior but when he looked inside, he immediately went into his demented routine: snarling, jumping up and down, kicking the oven, grabbing me by the throat. I got angry. I considered kicking the bastard in the bollocks, but the idea of doing six months solitary for this singular pleasure? Forget it. After a severe shaking, I got thrown to the floor.

"Duc El Baraka needs oven now to bake bread," the irritating Ollier informed me, in his birdlike voice. "You must work harder. Finish cleaning in ten minutes."

Behind Ollier, the gorilla rumbled and shook like Krakatoa.

So, once more into the breach, I crawled headfirst inside the oven. I bit my tongue to quell the panic crawling through me and, despite the high temperature, my whole body broke out in an ice-cold sweat. I started to retch. Just ten more minutes, I told myself. Ten more minutes and I'll be done with this hellhole.

With eyes clenched, I chipped and jabbed at the vitrified filth. After five minutes the demons of claustrophobia yelled in my ear, telling me I was being buried alive. Entombed. Horror overwhelmed me. I had to get out, and involuntarily I shouted out for my mummy as I tried to wriggle in retreat, but couldn't. Someone – the gorilla, no doubt – had grabbed my ankles and, with tremendous force, was pushing my whole body back into the oven.

I tried to kick but the grip simply tightened and quashed my attempts. I pushed against the back wall of the oven with all my strength, but to no avail. My arms buckled under the immense force, thrusting against me. I yelled for help but my voice simply reverberated, trapped within the oven. My legs then jack-knifed and I heard the oven door slam shut with a loud metallic clang.

The dark darkened, black as death. I railed, smashing at the door with my feet – but it was immovable, latched from the outside.

When one is suddenly placed in a situation of extreme danger, staring into the mouth of death, the mind transcends fear and panic and achieves, in an instant, a blissful calm. With eyes closed, at peace with myself, a silent movie of my life and family began to flicker in the theatre of my mind. I saw myself playing football on the streets of Bethnal Green; walking to school holding my raw onion and sugar sandwiches; playing hide and seek and British Bulldog in the school playground…

My reverie came to a sudden end when the gas burner to the side of me burst into flame.

Holy Moly Mother of God, I'm going to be roasted alive.

I saw the ovens at Auschwitz, people being burned down to the skeleton, and I screamed. The hot air seared my throat, only a pathetic rasping noise being emitted. Although the blue flames were low, the heat increased dramatically and my nasal passages dried up. The liqueous coating on my eyes evaporated, so that blinking became impossible. I could smell my prison clothes and hair starting to scorch.

Perhaps I'm blessed with gallows humour or perhaps it was a prelude to my death, but I started laughing, viewing myself from above. All squashed up in a fucking oven in a Paris prison just seemed a ludicrous way to die. Wait 'til Tony the Greek hears about this, it'll give the gang a right old laugh, I thought. Alan went to Paris on a day trip doing a drug run and ended up getting cooked medium-rare by some geezer called Duc El Baraka in a Paris nick.

I was still laughing when the oven door suddenly opened and I was violently hauled out. The gorilla, Ollier, a screw and a few of the plongeurs watched in amazement as I just stood there, chuckling and smouldering.

The screw ordered me to follow him.

Climbing the stairwell, the guard informed me that I had a court appearance at 9am. He escorted me to the washroom. I stripped and took one of La Santé's infamous dribbling showers; I was so thirsty, I drank most of the allotted water. I got clean work clothes and was taken back to Cell 336. It was after lights out, so everyone was asleep, their whistles and snores punctuating the heavy breathing.

I lay on the top bunk and snuggled into the straw mattress. Due to the day's exertions I fell asleep in seconds. It wasn't a deep sleep, because I woke up constantly, watching the night-guard chain-smoking on the landing. Poor bastard was as much a prisoner as us prisoners – held captive by his job, in prison night after night, his life ticking away in boredom as he developed lung cancer.

Pierre had diarrhoea and was discharging his bowels every two hours, with savage grunts and spurting noises I found funny until I remembered it was my turn to do the slopping out in the morning.

Sleep and dreams came and went, dissolved and then reformed, until...

Clackety-clack-clackety-clack. Clackety-clack-clackety-clack.

I had to wait for the paddy wagon to take me to the courthouse. Slopping out that morning had almost topped my list of disgusting jobs I'd done, but not quite. That dubious honour went to my past employment as a chicken plucker at Irmin's Halal butcher's. Irmin's was in a narrow alley of tenements behind Wentworth Street: a row of dilapidated, Dickensian lodging houses and slummy businesses, all leaning together, tottering, as though close to collapse. They were home to Irish navvies, tin cup peddlers, prostitutes, cliques of foreigners, cobblers, and rag and bone men. It was a rackety place living on the edge of destitution.

Irmin's sold only chickens, hundreds a day. The chickens arrived live every morning, from a farm somewhere in Buckinghamshire. Each basket contained twenty chickens packed beak to butt, like winged sardines. Irmin's order was always the same: twelve baskets, two hundred and forty birds. We'd unload the wire baskets from the lorry, with the chickens screeching, shitting and crowing with fright. Then we'd stack the poor sods inside the shop on a long bench, in two rows, six baskets each. Mr Irmin would then meticulously sharpen his knife and strew sawdust all over the floor. He'd say a prayer in Yiddish before opening the concertina of wooden shutters at the entrance. The shop was then open for business, with customers already lining up, mostly the Indian and Pakistani restaurant owners.

These customers would scurry up and down the cages, eyeballing the chickens, pulling out any bird that caught their fancy, grabbing its legs as they yanked it from the cage. To do this inexpertly could mean a sharp peck on the hand or worse, with the bird escaping in an explosion of feathers and thrashing wings, off up the alley. Mr Irmin didn't take kindly to losing profits and would flash his carving knife menacingly, spouting a fusillade of Hebrew and English insults at the offender, and he always got paid in full.

After the customer chose his chickens, he'd hand them to Mr Irmin, who, standing at a large galvanised drum, would swiftly slit the bird's throat and let the blood drain into the drum. Its head lolling, the chicken would be thrown onto a table where us chicken-pluckers (there were two) got plucking; yanking feathers off the bird at incredible speed, we'd strip the feathers downwards towards the feet, until the flesh was nude.

As the feathers came off and the chicken turned cold in death, all kinds of horrible ticks and fleas abandoned ship. The fleas, apart from being irritating, didn't bite but, by some sixth sense or instinct, they headed immediately back to the cages to feast on the other, live, chickens. The ticks, degenerate parasites, were far less fussy. They'd scurry up fingers and arms to find the damp, hot flesh of armpits and then move to your crotch. They'd burrow painfully beneath the skin, to spend their days languidly sipping at the passing blood flow. The only successful extermination of the tick was extremely painful: place a lit cigarette directly onto the dug-in critter, and then burn the bastard to death.

Naked, tick- and flea-less, the poor chicken now got slung over to the trimmer, who – with cleaver blurring – hacked off the head and neck, slit open the backside and gutted the bird by hand. Then he chopped off its legs, gave the carcass a final once-over with a blue-flamed Bunsen burner that singed off broken quills and the detritus of feathers. He'd wrap the chicken and all its dismembered parts in newspaper and hand the lot to the customer.

The whole operation took less than six minutes.

At the height of the slaughter, the air became a Jackson Pollock of guts, shit, feathers, fleas, ticks, slippery livers, beaks, tongues, heads, maggot-laying flies, crazy dogs, parasitic worms, loud housewives and, most of all, blood everywhere. By five in the afternoon, every worker glistened with chicken blood; was freckled with chicken blood; ended up smeared, daubed, greased, soaked in blood. Exhausted, we'd all troop across the street to the Bunch of Grapes for a pint, proudly wearing our red badges of courage, stinking of chicken shit and gizzards.

Palethorpe was waiting for me in an interview room at the courthouse. He greeted me with an absurd display of bonhomie, lots of hugging and hand-pumping that I immediately construed as fake. He's probably going to break some awful news, I thought. I've been condemned to life without parole.

I was totally wrong.

"Sit down, young man, sit down," he effused. Not waiting for me to sit down, he gushed on. "The charges of drug trafficking, causing an explosion, being a member of the OAS, they have all now been dropped."

Well, you could have knocked me down with one of Mr Irmin's chicken feathers. Hearing those words had me winging out of the Santé, soaring above Paris, sweeping across the Channel, gyring over London and then swooping along the Roman Road into The Wheatsheaf. There I ordered myself a nice, frothy sherbert, a pickled onion and a plate of shepherd's pie from the barmaid, Rena. She was giving me the eye, her tits heaving out of her low-cut blouse as she slid her tongue lasciviously over her pouted, painted lips, getting all my hormones standing to attention...

Palethorpe torpedoed my reverie.

"However," he began. "Entering France illegally on a forged British passport is a very serious crime, one which could carry a minimum sentence of a year. Tomorrow, at 10am, you will be interviewed regarding these charges by detectives at the Police Judiciaire, 7th Arrondissment."

Back at La Santé, I decided to keep mum about Palethorpe's good news. In prison, the heavier the crime, the more respect you get from other inmates. Demoting myself to doing time for using a bent passport would've had about as much cachet as a fart in a thunderstorm; anyway, I liked being seen as an arty beatnik, a mad dog of an Englishman, in league with the OAS, hell-bent on nothing less than the destruction of la République française.

When I got to the cellblock landing, the place was a hive of frantic activity. Inmates were scrubbing and cleaning the floors and walls of their cells. Screws ran up and down the corridors like a herd of elephants, yelling ceaseless orders and when they descended, en masse, into a cell, they would scream, "Pigsty, pigsty!" and then they'd throw bedding, clothes, and the inmates out onto the landing as they conducted a search for knives, alcohol and drugs.

At 336, I learned all this dementia was going down because the Governor and board members of the prison were undertaking their annual surprise tour of the facility, so the Warden wanted the cellblock all ship-shape and shinola.

"They'll give us a good lunch today," mused Jean. "Maybe steak and *pommes frites.*"

"Yeah, so we can all tell the Governor how well fed and humanely treated we are," countered Pierre. "God help any zany bastard who complains, the Warden will have him hung, drawn and quartered."

In a clatter of boots and batons, the screws tumbled into 336 and herded us onto the landing while they searched the cell. A gut-curdling feeling of dread leadened over me: a fear that the screws would find a weapon such as a sharpened nail or file in our cell. It would mean instant solitary for all of us. Fortunately they didn't. But, as we were filing back into the cell, the Warden yelled at me.

"You, Artist. Get your fanny down to the kitchen. *Vite, vite!*" He pushed his way through the guards and prodded me in the ribs with his baton. "*Vite, vite!*" he yelled in my ear.

One of the guards nelsoned my arm in a bone-crushing grip, then double-timed me down the stairwell, into the labyrinths of the prison.

Cooking lunch for the Governor and his entourage had heightened the sense of panic and pandemonium in the

kitchen. The noise was fearful, the disorder frenetic – a pigsty of squealing and yelling. The staff raged and cursed, flitting like phantoms through the flames and steam. I saw them hacking at meats, skinning onions, cleaving cabbages. The dishwashers staggered among regiments of filthy saucepans and piled totteries of plates, overwhelmed. On the floor, strewn rubbish festered and thickened by the minute, providing mouldering camouflage for the rats and cockroaches. The heat here was brutal. The breath of the great ovens sweltered the choking air, turning it to an unbreathable and sweaty syrup, exascerbated still further by explosions of grease that sent geysers of flame and showering sparks everywhere. It was a hellish and brutish scene, centred upon Duc El Baraka, standing at a great butcher's block. He was barking orders, blaspheming, vilifying, windmilling his huge Popeye arms, cleavering the flesh of a quartered horse.

I moved into the darkest shadows of the kitchen, keeping out of sight, standing in a vaulted recess and hoping to be no more than a spectator. It wasn't to be. Olliers saw me and hurried over to whisper to the Duc. Then he snailed my way, in his curious mode of locomotion that reminded me of an amoeba.

"English, you're late," squealed Olliers in his tasty little voice. "You were due here at 8am."

"I was in court."

"No excuse," he said, handing me a bristle-bare broom. "Sweep the floors. Put all the rubbish in those dustbins."

He pointed to three bins along a wall, each already overflowing with festering rubbish.

"Empty the bins upstairs in the pig truck," he went on. "When the floors are clean, sawdust them. Now get on with it – in three hours the Governor will inspect the kitchen. God forbid if he cannot eat off the floor, because the Duc will personally castrate you."

And I believed him. So, under threat of being made able to sing castrato, for two hours I shoved the broom around the kitchen and under sinks. I swept between ovens, behind sacks accumulating the muck into a small mountain of oozy sludge.

It was hard work but the worst was yet to come.

The first dustbin weighed a ton. I had to drag it up a circular stone stairwell, a hundred and fifty steps in all, across a fenced courtyard to a lorry. I then had to lift the bin onto my shoulder and dump it into the back of the vehicle, which, when it was full, went on its way to a pig farm somewhere north of Paris.

It took ten dustbins to empty the kitchen of its filthy refuse; ten muscle-wrenching, back-breaking journeys up the gloomy steps to the courtyard. On the fifth or sixth trek, my muscles protesting and fingers bloodied, my hero Marshall came to mind with a brilliant plan.

It was 1944; Marshall had been captured by the Nazis on a secret mission to Paris, and then taken to the headquarters of the Gestapo for questioning. Despite all his tantric training, he knew that, unless he escaped, eventually the Germans would break him or kill him. Just like me, he was given the chore of cleaning the kitchens and emptying the rubbish in a truck. After depositing the last bin, Marshall checked the disposition of the guards nonchalantly, before climbing into the back of the truck and squirrelling himself beneath the rubbish. After half an hour, the truck's driver checked the load; the army guards opened the gates and the truck chugged out of Gestapo headquarters to Melliers, forty miles north of Paris. There, Marshall alighted from the vehicle and contacted the Resistance. He got back to London via a British submarine from Deauville.

What a plan.

After dumping my final load, if the opportunity arose I thought I'd follow Marshall's example and hide in the back of the lorry to make my escape. By the tenth load, though, I was physically exhausted, suffering from giddiness and nausea, shaking in every limb. This last load, almost twice the weight of the others, repulsed me. It was full of bit-parts of a slaughtered horse – the head, hooves and endless ropes of innards oozing a grey-green liquid.

When I finally emerged into the courtyard the truck was gone, and with it the possibility to escape.

Back in the kitchen I wandered around sprinkling sawdust everywhere. The fever of cooking the Governor's lunch was reaching its noisy, frantic climax. Great meat plates were loaded with thick horse steaks, while bowls of boiled potatoes stood heating in the steam ovens, along with chopped cabbage and whole, boiled onions. Screws were directing a few workers to carry heated plates and sauce boats of gravy up to the Governor's dining room.

The Duc's mad face gleamed by oven light, drenched with sweat and blood. On his butcher's block lay a chateaubriand – this, the finest filet steak, was for the Governor and his few guests. All the horse steaks were for the screws. As I continued sawdusting, I witnessed a scene that made me wonder if I hadn't descended a ladder into the very belly of Hell, to meet the Devil himself. The *Sturm und Drang* of the kitchen's culinary opera was reaching its zenith with everyone working in a state of manic agitation, all baying. The gorilla, perhaps fevered by the intense heat or drunk, seemed to be possessed of spirits; seeing demons or angels, his eyes rolled around in their sockets in an alarming way. Spittle coated his lips and his voice had acquired a multiple personality: one minute cooing and whorishly suggestive, the next bellowing like a stuck pig and then barking scatter-brained orders in a military manner.

With great ceremony the gorilla held up the chateaubriand above his head, like a prizefighter would a trophy belt. His tirade lasted for five minutes. The only words I understood were "Gouverneur Soutine et Madame Soutine!" Holding the meat in one hand, he repeated "le Gouverneur" over and over, and then began punching the meat with a clenched fist, smashing the flesh with tremendous force and splattering blood everywhere. Now, as the bruised meat swelled with blood, he smeared it across his chest and rubbed it into the black gauze of hair under his armpits and down his arms. Finally, he hawked snot from his nose and spat on the meat, saying "le Gouverneur". Then he roared with laughter, and everyone applauded. The Duc then took a bottle of brandy that was standing on the oven to flambé the roasted chateaubriand, and downed a massive dose of it. Slightly weaving, he let out a long, harrowing hyena-like laugh, until the veins bulged in knots at his temples and his pupils rolled upward until only the whites of his eyes showed.

He yelled at us in a tone of disgust. "Madame Soutine," he grimaced, spitting the words out as though they had a disgusting taste. "Bitch."

This was greeted with much laughter, so he repeated it. "Bitch! Whore!"

Taking the meat in both hands he bent it into a V-shape and began sticking his tongue into the fold of the flesh, licking it lasciviously, slobbering in the process, cooing and muttering. "*Ma chérie, Madame Soutine, j'adore!*" he simpered, much to everyone's delight.

The gorilla then trembled violently, with sweat bursting from every pore and matting the thick carpet of hair on his body. He threw off his apron, untied his cotton chef's pants and put the chateaubriand inside.

He held it onto to his genitals.

My mind was doing mental gymnastics, trying to believe what I was seeing in this madhouse. A new voice emerged from the Duc, a gentle lover's whisper. "*Ma chérie, mon amour.*" Slowly, his huge hips and vast rump began to rotate, to gyrate, to fornicate the meat, faster and faster, heaving in and out as little sobs escaped from his mouth. These were followed by gasps and grunts as the tempo of his carnal copulation increased, until he let out a long orgiastic moan. He shuddered and an ear-to-ear grin divided his fat face.

Everyone stared at the Duc. Dumbstruck. Silent. He opened his eyes and started to laugh as he took the meat from his pants, threw it onto the grill, seared it, oiled it – and then tossed it into the oven to roast. Ten minutes later, the gorilla fished the chateaubriand from the oven, spat on it for luck, put it on a hot meat dish and handed it to a worker who headed upstairs with it at full speed to the Governor's office.

All was now calm in the kitchen, with the chefs and *plongeurs* helping themselves to horse steaks and boiled onions. Much to my surprise, the repulsive Olliers invited me to eat. I got steak and potatoes and, again, Olliers surprised me by fetching me a glass of wine, saying I'd done a good job of cleaning the kitchen.

I salivated at the idea of my first good meal since I'd left London. But it wasn't to be. More drama was about to unfold. The gorilla, not only deranged now but drunk, swept the food from my plate, sending the steak and potatoes skidding into the sawdust.

"You eat on the floor. Quickly now, doll face," he said in French. "Quickly!"

Laughing, the bastard grabbed hold of my neck and with tremendous strength forced me to the floor, pushing my face into the steak.

"Eat my little dog," he growled. "Eat!"

"The Governor's on his way down," Olliers yelled.

The Duc let go of me and dashed into the cloakroom to change into clean pants and apron, while everyone else skittered like cockroaches to their posts and pretended to be working intently.

After a tense five minutes the Governor didn't show. Olliers, full of hangdog embarrassment, apologised to the gorilla. I had a feeling Olliers had lied to save me. Eventually the Governor, accompanied by Madame Soutine, the prison doctor M. Etienne, board members of the prison, and the Warden with several guards in tow, did visit the kitchen. They did a perfunctory tour and finally the Governor and his entourage circled the Duc.

"Chef Baraka," enthused the Governor. "Lunch was excellent, the chateaubriand fit for a king."

It took a monumental collective effort from the kitchen staff not to burst out laughing.

"One man's meat is another man's mistress," mumbled the drunk Le Duc, groping for words as he hid his brandied breath behind his hand.

Befuddled by the Duc's statement, the Governor and his group departed. By eight, the kitchen was closed down for the night and all of the workers and kitchen hands had returned to their cells, except for me. The Duc insisted I finish cleaning a mess of tin trays and mixing bowls, while he sat on his fat arse watching me, drinking red wine, getting shit-faced. Using a mixture of sand and a sludgy bar of carbolic soap with cold water, I laboriously scrubbed and rubbed, polished and buffed until – after an hour's hard work – the job was done.

The gorilla, still drunk and glugging from a bottle of Pernod, came and stood unsteadily next to me. He stunk like a slaughterhouse. He nodded his approval at the tin trays and pans I'd cleaned, then grinned an inebriated goofy grin, like a big fat baby. He put his cumbrous arm round my shoulder and squeezed me affectionately.

"Now vee go to washroom, take shower together."

His grip tightened on my shoulder; the muscles of my sphincter tightened as well. Stumblefooted, the Duc, holding me in a python-like grip, picked up a tray of uncooked meats and we staggered over to the cold room.

Inside the temperature plummeted to an arctic 28° F (-2° C). Frosted sides of beef and rictus grinning pigs hung from the ceiling. On the floor were trays full of rabbits, chickens and every organ imaginable; tripe, lungs, kidneys, hearts, liver – even a box of cows' eyes, looking like melancholic marbles. Very quickly, we both began to shiver violently. An hour in this place would freeze a man solid.

The Duc tried to lift the tray of meat onto a shelf with one hand, but it proved too heavy and he let go of me to use both hands. I ducked under his arm and leapt towards the heavy metal door. The Duc panicked and grabbed my hair, pulling me backwards. I slipped on the box of cows' eyes and skidded over, crashing heavily into the wall, sending eyeballs bouncing across the floor.

Now, as the leering Duc moved to wrap me in his fleshy arms, he too slipped on the bovine eyeballs and keeled over. He bounced to the ground like a downed dirigible. Frightened for my life, I scrambled out of the cold store and bolted the door behind me – only just in time, as the Duc began to bludgeon against it.

Halfway up the dark yawn of the stairwell, it occurred to me the gorilla could freeze to death and, with the door bolted, it wouldn't take a Maigret to suss that I did it. So, cautiously, I went back down to the kitchen. All was deathly quiet. I put my ear to the door and could hear heavy, snarly snoring. Warily, I withdrew the bolt and peeked inside the cold room. The Duc lay on the floor like a jolly snowman fast asleep, his whole flabby body dusted with particles of ice. He was gripping an empty bottle of Pernod. I dragged him to the kitchen – not an easy task, like manhandling a beached whale – and then covered his body with potato sacks.

In a bin on a workbench, I found leftover steaks; in the chef's locker, four bottles of French beer. And so, for half an hour, I pigged and chug-a-lugged out, to the accompaniment of the Duc's leviathan snoring. When I got up to the landing, I informed the night-guard that the head chef was drunk and asleep in the kitchen, so after unlocking Cell 336 he went downstairs to investigate.

I climbed into my bunk, slightly drunk, and fell straight to sleep.

At the Police Judiciaire on Rue Thoreau, I met with Palethorpe and two chain-smoking detectives. It was a scene straight out of a Mickey Spillane thriller: dark room, single-bulbed desk lamp burning my eyes, and the dicks sucking on Gauloises, constantly blowing smoke in my face.

"Aldridge, the police insist you stand trial for illegal entry into France," said Palethorpe, summing up the situation. "This carries a minimum of a six-month prison sentence. The false passport will be dealt with by the British courts when you return to England. The problem is, the judiciary system here in Paris is overloaded with cases waiting to go to trial. As a consequence, you could be in La Santé a year before your case is heard."

The only thing I could think of was that somewhere in the world, there must be someone worse off than me – but right at that moment, I didn't think so. It felt like I'd hit rock bottom again.

"However," continued Palethorpe with emphasis, as though he was about to pull a rabbit out of a hat, "I will make a plea to the police that, rather than keep you locked up at taxpayers' expense, they declare you persona non grata and then extradite you back to England."

In the meat wagon heading back to La Santé, I realised I hadn't a clue what persona non grata meant – or extradite. I felt about as happy as a gravedigger at a baptism.

Chapter Six

It was Jean's last night in jail. In the cell, we pressured him to tell us about his adventures in the gigolo business: the sex, drugs and debauchery; his conquests and casualties among the blue-blood set of Europe's high society. Had Jean screwed any princesses, duchesses or dowagers of the British Empire? Which royals had he squirrelled off for secret trysts of fornication?

I guess we all imagined his life to be full of gorgeous chicks, luxury yachts, hot nightclubs and sex, all of it constantly fuelled by the finest champagnes, wines and pharmaceuticals. As we were to learn, though, the truth was very different: Jean was a conundrum, a paradox beyond our imaginings. At first, whether out of humility or not wishing to betray clients and confidences, he refused to discuss his lifestyle, his boudoir accomplishments. We persisted, particularly Tali, who, facing a life sentence, needed all the titillation he could get.

Finally, Jean relented. In a voice hushed with confidentiality, he began to talk.

"People's vision of a gigolo borders on the mythological – fuelled, I suspect, by the notion that we're all Casanovas," he said. "Well, we're not. In fact, the bacteriological combustion of fucking – the slimy exchange of bodily fluids with strangers – abhors me."

What the hell does that mean? I thought.

"Sure," he went on, "my business sounds glamorous, but it's a business. Cash is my orgasm." He paused. "I once had a date with the world's richest woman."

Tali immediately squawked. "Elizabeth Taylor?"

"No, it's Queen something-or-other," said Pierre. "She's got oodles of oil money."

Jean shook his head.

"Queen Elizabeth," I blurted out, with little confidence I'd be right. I wasn't.

"The Maharani of Maghadon. There's a song about how rich she is," quipped Roger.

"Mrs Howard Hughes," ventured Andre.

"Howard Hughes never married," I corrected him.

"Brigitte Bardot," offered Roger in desperation.

"The Hotel Plaza Athénée is just a couple of miles from this prison," said Jean. "I'm at The English Bar, a watering hole for the rich and famous. I'm dressed in black pinstripe threads – double-breasted, of course – hand-tailored, at Burke's of Saville Row. Didn't cost me a franc, bought by a lady friend simply because I had afternoon tea with her at The Ritz in London. I'm drinking Glenlivet with spring water, smoking a hand-rolled Cohiba cigar. I sit at a corner table, where I have the whole bar in view... Imagine me, if you will, as a lion at the edge of a watering hole in the jungle, waiting for my prey. I'm not interested in any healthy species of the human animal, just the sick. The sicker, the better. Close to death? Better still."

A chill shivered through me. What I'd hoped for, a story with a few laughs, was sounding more like a voyage into the dark heart of the human psyche.

"The drink and cigar are free, courtesy of the barman. Why?" asked Jean.

"Because he thinks you're cute."

"You jerked him off the night before."

"You touch your toes for him."

"You're servicing his bitch of a wife."

"He's in on my scam, the act," revealed Jean. "His name is Walter. He knows, if I meet a woman, sooner or later she'll order – or get me to order – champagne, and he'll get a good tip. *Comprenez-vous, mes amis?* So, I watch and wait. Patience is my virtue. During any evening when I'm working, beautiful women throw me provocative glances and flash erotic smiles. They offer nothing. A middle-aged woman comes into the bar, alone, I don't notice her at first, but feel a frisson – an electric current, like a tremor through the room. People stare at her, then lean into each other and whisper. Obviously, she is famous – but I don't immediately recognise her."

"It's Two-Ton Tessie O'Shea," quipped Tali.

Jean ignored this stupid remark and continued. "Now I begin to focus in on her. She sits at the bar and orders a champagne cocktail. Her suit is Balenciaga; the watch, Patek Philippe; her necklace of emeralds, by Van Cleef and Arpels. But it's the eyes I focus on, I've seen those eyes in all the places the wealthy haunt... They're buyers' eyes. See, there's only two kinds of people in the world, the buyers and the bought."

He turned to me. "Alan," he said. "You're bought. You've got a job, you get paid a salary, you're bought... This woman, though, she buys whatever, who ever she wants. She has more money than sense. I'm stimulated. And so begins the hunt. Before the night is out, I will have stripped her naked to the bone and eaten her heart out."

"We coming to the sexy bits?" asked Tali.

Again, Jean ignored the remark. "Walter talks to the lady," he said. "If he doesn't know who she is, he'll find out. He'll ask her where she's from. Is she staying at the hotel? If not, where? Will her husband be joining her? All this information he will pass on to me. Why?"

No-one responded.

"Because he'll get well paid for it. After two cocktails, the lady moves on, to Bourbon. She's been in the bar less than twenty minutes. She doesn't nurse drinks but throws them down, an alcoholic – and so she reveals a second weakness. Tali, what was the first?"

Tali looked totally bemused. "The champagne cocktail."

"No wonder blacks become pimps and never gigolos. A bar stool opens up next to her. The hunt begins. I go sit next to her. I acknowledge her politely, nothing overt, I'm not into all that teasy-weasy boudoir bullshit because it bores me. She pulls a cigarette from a carton of Pall Mall, doesn't use an expensive cigarette case. This tells me two things: she's a heavy smoker, and impatient. She hasn't time to unload a carton of cigarettes into a fancy case. She's on a sixty-a-day habit. Smokes for herself, not to be sociable.

"I could've whipped out my Dupont and lit her cigarette, but it was too obvious. Instead, she offers me a cigarette. I take it and let Walter light us both up. See, guys, there's a chess game opening up here. Information on my opponent is paramount. If I'm going to spend approximately eight hours with her, then if I have insights into her obsessions, behavioural patterns and fears, it gives me an advantage. To get laid is not an objective here for me. To accumulate wealth is.

"It's information that brings the lion to its prey, watching a herd of water buffalo, searching for one that limps, is sick or slow or newborn. When he chooses which one to attack, it will be because he knows he only has to expend minimum energy on the kill. I'm the same."

I was sure we were all starting to regret asking Jean about his exploits. We'd expected sordid stories of sex, after all – not a bleeding lecture on lions.

"Her eyes are masterpieces of pain, of loneliness. Buyers' eyes, she gets whatever she wants with a chequebook. She buys people, buys sex – but she can't buy love. She introduces herself simply as Barbara. The name allied to the face sends telegraphic messages along the synapses of my brain into my memory banks. There is a familiarity about her, but I can't recall from where or when.

"We small-talk for half an hour. I learn she's been married five times – must be American – and has a son who races cars. She loves Tangiers, has five houses and is in Paris buying an apartment. She invites me to have dinner at her hotel.

"There's an old maxim – take the obvious and reverse it, well, now was the time to apply it. The obvious would be to go with her, have dinner, fine wine in the best of the luxury hotels in Paris. But, there would be no intrigue. No challenge in that. So I tell her no, I have dinner plans but that she can join me if she wishes. For a few seconds I can see the chemistry of panic ripple outwards from her eyes – she's not used to being refused – but she accepts. I take her to Prunier on Rue Duphot. As we leave the bar, Walter hands me a slip of paper, which I fold and tuck into my waistcoat pocket without reading it.

"At the restaurant I order turbot accompanied by an ice-chilled bottle of Grand Cru Montrachet 1957. She has an interest in poetry. I quote her Verlaine, Rimbaud. When she speaks I become her eunuch, a slave to each word, giving everything she says my devoted attention. I listen intently, as this pathetic little rich girl spews out her woes. I worship at the altar of her gossip. Slowly, a rarefied chemistry begins working; those green eyes, the green of dollar bills, lose their boredom. They spiral with a vapid sensuality and, above the Chanel perfume, I can smell the sexual musk from the moist darkness of her most secret place."

All our eyes lit up. We'd never heard pussy described like that. Maybe, finally, we were reaching the good bits.

"Now she becomes anxious. Like all American women, she has no sensuality. With them, it's all wham bam, thank you, ma'am. She gropes at my crotch and again suggests we go to The Ritz for a nightcap. Again, I tell her I have plans and she is welcome to join me. We drive across town to Avenue de Choisy in the 13th Arrondissement, to a small restaurant, Tang's. The owner, a friend, escorts us through a labyrinth of corridors to a tiny room laid with cushions and shrouded in silk drapes.

"I smoke opium. She has no hesitation in joining me. After a soporific hour, I return her to The Ritz. Everyone – concierge, front desk, and bellboys – bows before her. They use her surname. I'm with the richest woman in the world. Of course, she has the Presidential Suite – it's huge and vulgar, like barroom baroque. She orders Cristal, gets into a silk dressing gown. I suggest a hot bath. It'll make her sleepy. I've brought opium with me. I can't believe it: she phones room service to get her bath ready. Two maids arrive. They run a bath, lay towels on the floor. When they leave I smoke some opium and she takes some hits, inexpertly inhaling far too much smoke. She strips naked and her flesh reminds me of dead chicken.

"The champagne arrives. I tell the butler to bring a bottle of Louis XIII Brandy. He's back in no time, his legs fuelled by the thought of a big tip. I mix half brandy, half champagne and bring it to her in the bathroom. She stands naked in the bath and toasts me. Her sexuality was pathetic: screw me and go. We both toss our drinks down. I wrap her in several towels and she leads me to the cavernous bedroom. I ask her if she'd like a bennie, guaranteed to have us bouncing off the walls until dawn. She laughs lasciviously. We both take one, only hers isn't an amphetamine but a narcotic. Mine is just chalk. After twenty minutes, she's fast asleep. I take the Patek Philippe watch; the necklace; a billfold with 330,000 francs; a Cartier bracelet.

"We were together five hours. I drove my Maserati all night, got to Cannes by 10am, drove on to Monte Carlo, fenced the night's take and was in bed at the Hotel de Paris, $47,000 richer by midday."

We sat in silence, our visions of a gigolo gone totally awry.

The following morning, after breakfast, Jean said his goodbyes. He and I embraced.

"Alan, when you get out of this hellhole, come down to Cannes. To the Carlton. See Albert or Jimmy, long-time barman there, they know where to find me. Come. Relax, get tanned. Maybe I teach you more about the gigolo business. You'd be good. I'll be your pimp."

We laughed.

"Silence!" yelled the screw.

"Fuck you," said Jean, and walked out to freedom.

At two in the afternoon, I got summoned to the Police Judiciaire at Rue Thoreau, and went across town in the meat-wagon. Palethorpe was waiting for me in the foyer. He looked like he'd wet his pants, all agitated and flustered. We went to an interview room, where the guard took my handcuffs off and then left.

Palethorpe smiled.

"How about dinner tonight, ol' boy?" he asked. "Les Deux Magots. Great food and bohemian clientele. Right up your alley."

The penny didn't drop. I just stared back at Palethorpe blankly.

"You're free, dear boy," he beamed, and shook my hand.

My mind raced, flipping at tremendous speed through the events of the past ten – or was it eleven? – days, until it reached the present moment.

"Free!" I yelled.

Palethorpe nodded. "The French have dropped all charges. However, on a damper note, the government has issued a warrant of persona non grata against you, which means you have twenty-four hours to get out of the country. You can be escorted onto a plane back to London. Once there, you will face a charge of being in possession of a counterfeit passport. Alternatively, you can choose to be escorted out of the country by the police to any of France's bordering countries: Belgium, Luxembourg, Switzerland, Germany, Spain and Italy."

"How about Monaco?"

This took Palethorpe by surprise. He didn't know the answer. "I'll find out and let you know later," he said. "Now you'll go back to La Santé and release papers will be prepared. You could be drinking a glass of wine in a Parisian bistro by dusk."

I hugged Palethorpe, and danced a jig of joy around him.

Back in the cell I blurted out my good news.

"Hey, guys – I'll be cruisin' the Boulevard tonight, eyeballing the ladies, downing a few pints and with luck, a pair of knickers too."

I laughed but no-one else did. They all stared at me with hostile expressions.

"You geeky-looking twat," snapped Tali finally. "The Warden's been giving us hell all morning because of you."

"Wha'd I do?"

"He says you kicked the shit out of the head chef last night – left him good as dead in the kitchen. Screws found him this morning, gnawed by rats. Poor bastard's in the hospital and his friend the Warden's not very happy with you."

"Leave it off. The fat tub of lard came on to me, drunk out of his gourd – attacked me, slipped and knocked himself out.

Anyway, I told the screw on duty last night that he was down in the kitchen, unconscious."

"Yeah, tell that to the Warden. He's been up here twice, looking for you. First time, he and his goons turned the cell over, made a right mess. No sooner we get the place tidy, back he comes and makes us slop-out every cell on the landing. Then he came back just five minutes ago, had us all out of the cell, then he went through your bed space with a fine-tooth comb, like he was looking for stashed drugs, ciggies, anything illegal so's to put you in solitary."

Suddenly an intuitive voice whispered a warning that I was being set up: maybe the Warden wasn't looking, but planting. I broke out in a cold sweat at the idea, and began hurriedly groping through the straw stuffing of my mattress.

Without warning the Warden, with three screws in tow, appeared at the cell door...

Just as my fingers closed over the cold metal of a blade.

"All you faggots, out!" yelled the Warden, unlocking the door. I had no choice but to grab the blade and conceal it in my hand as we were herded out onto the landing. I dreaded to think what the penalty would be for an inmate carrying a concealed weapon.

Out on the landing I began to shake.

After ten minutes of frantic mayhem, tearing the cell apart, the Warden emerged from the cell and faced us. He looked like he'd just shit a watermelon, obviously pissed at not finding the planted blade.

"All right, you clever fags, slags, queers and queens," he thundered. "Get in two lines – NOW!"

Like lobotomised rats, the eight of us shuffled into two ragged rows of four. I purposefully positioned myself to be the last in line. With the blade palmed in my hand, I needed all the time and divine inspiration I could get to make it disappear. My legs were shaking violently, though not noticeably because of my baggy prison pants, but I was sure every screw on the landing could hear the booming palpitations of my panicked heart.

So much for Palethorpe's prediction that I'd be cruising the boulevards tonight. Yet again, fate's unsuspecting path had taken another sharp turn and I was minutes from being busted for possession of a lethal weapon, getting a severe kicking from the Warden and being thrown in solitary, for God knows how long.

The shakedown of my cellmates was extraordinarily rapid, almost inconsequential. It was as if the Warden knew in advance I was guilty as hell.

Now it was my turn. The Warden grinned malevolently as I limped and shuffled before him. He bellowed a mouthful of Arabic and an Algerian boy, a worker everyone called The Fruit, weaselled his way between the screws and stood grinning his retarded grin next to the Warden. The Fruit sold drugs, cigarettes, and food, even sex to the inmates. He could take on a passive or active role, depending on the trick's coital proclivity. I'd seen the little bastard giving Pierre a bi-nightly hand-job for ten cigarettes a time. Now I wondered, what was his role in this Theatre of the Absurd I found myself in?

The body search began with the Warden grabbing my ears, snapping my head down and rifling through my hair vigorously with his salami-like fingers. The purpose of this, obviously, was not to find a blade but to make me look ridiculous, with my hair sticking out, unkempt and scarecrowish. Next, he plunged his callused hands inside my shirt and frisked my chest, back and armpits. Removing his hands he checked my arms, forced open my hands and then grabbed my family jewels. With a wicked grin, he yanked them down, hard. Excruciating pain jagged through my body as tears popped from my eyes.

The Fruit laughed. "Big boys don't cry, big boys don't cry!" he shouted.

One day I hoped I'd bump into this facetious little git in a back alley. After I'd finished with him, he'd be no oil painting – well, maybe a Picasso: his ears where his nose should be, his eyes looking up his own arsehole.

There were more indignities to come.

"Spread your legs," ordered the Warden.

I did, and he ran his hands round my privates, up my backside, then down my legs, looking increasingly puzzled.

"Bend over, touch your toes," he yelled, grabbing my head and jack-knifing me over, pulling my pants down.

All the inmates watching from the cells along the landing began to boo and bang their mugs on the bars, but the Warden was undeterred and ordered The Fruit to search my rectum.

"Me enjoy," squeaked The Fruit, shoving his fingers inside me, and then withdrawing them. "Nothing, " he squealed.

I pulled my pants up.

"Remove your shoes," ordered the Warden.

My shoes were prison-issue espadrilles without laces. You simply slipped them on and off, so I took a step backwards, leaving the shoes lying on the floor, looking and smelling like old kippers. Puzzlement flittered across the Warden's face and, with the angry noise from the inmates increasing in decibels by the second, he dismissed me. I slipped my shoes back on and shuffled back into the cell.

No-one talked. I said nothing about the blade, not knowing who I could trust, only hoping the Warden wouldn't return for another search, realising I had been extremely lucky to have fooled him.

When ordered onto the landing, I had the blade in the palm of my hand. As I waited in line to be frisked, I put it inside my pants, and then eased the blade down my leg until it emerged from the bottom and I concealed it under my shoe. When I stepped out of my espadrilles, the blade was concealed beneath the right shoe. When the Warden dismissed me, I simply put my feet back into the shoes and, keeping the blade under my right foot, limped and shuffled back into the cell. At the first opportunity I slipped the blade into the latrine. There'd be no slop-out until the next morning, and with luck I'd be long gone.

From lights out to the morning's predictable clackety-clack seemed an eternity, lying tensely awake on my bunk, expecting a shakedown with every passing minute. I'd doze off, only to fall into terrifying nightmares of solitary, its shapeless dark pressing all around me until, overwhelmed by its smothering blanket of claustrophobia, I'd wake up, screaming, and lie there sweating until again I'd find myself drifting down the corridors of sleep. This time I was greeted by gigantic fleas, each winking and leering at me, their sly little faces carbon copies of my own. To my horror, the vile creatures set on me, sawing into my flesh and drinking my blood until, emptied, I was no more than a skin-bag of bones...

I woke up to find myself being chewed on by bedbugs and fleas, feeling cockroaches skittering through my blankets. I prayed today would be my last in this hellish place. What if I did get out? I thought of Bethnal Green, its noisy trains chugging sulphurous smoke, dull rain on the dead streets, cold oozing up through the holes in my shoes, the spit and sawdust pubs with their stink of stale beer and influenza; and me, going back to my old job schlepping bananas off of rusty cargo boats down the West India Docks, fifty hours a week for a five pound pay packet. Then Jean came to mind, far south in the sunshine of the French Riviera, with the lick and slap of the Mediterranean grinding its ever-changing colours of moonlight and sunshine into the golden sands... Cannes and Saint-Tropez, where the girls had bodies like movie stars, wore just tans and bikinis, and sipped champagne, ice-cold, on the terraces of swank hotels that looked like baroque wedding cakes. Succumbing to this cinema-induced vision, I made the decision: if today's the day, I'm heading south.

Morning came, and breakfast, and slop-out. No sign of the Warden. After lunch, a screw came to the cell to escort me to the booking office.

I could smell freedom.

Palethorpe was there, waiting. He greeted me.

"Dear boy," he said. "We're finally getting you out of here, but lots of forms to sign first."

At least twenty needed my signature, and took half an hour. Then, the booking clerk couldn't find my clothes in storage, so I was given a very hairy, coarse three-piece suit of sackcloth that was extremely baggy and itchy. It made me look like a mental patient in Broadmoor.

"Now, Aldridge, do you intend going back to London? The only alternative the French authorities have offered is that you be escorted by the police to the German border at Strasbourg."

"I'll take Strasbourg," I responded without hesitation.

I had no idea where Strasbourg was, or cared. London held no allure, especially with the possibility of going to jail.

Palethorpe went through the release papers, writing Strasbourg as port of exit, then handed their considerable bulk over to a prison official who went into a delirium of red-rubber-stamping every sheet, putting copies into an envelope and handing them to Palethorpe.

I accompanied Palethorpe across a grim courtyard of ponderous architecture to a guardhouse next to huge wooden gates, beyond which lay Paris and freedom. Palethorpe handed the bulky envelope of discharge papers to the guard, who went through them meticulously, stamping each page, once with a black stamp for time and date, a second time with a red stamp showing the official badge of the French penal judiciare. It took half an hour. During this time I was getting extremely anxious, fearing the Warden would show up with some trumped-up charge that would put the kibosh on my getting released.

A doddery old gendarme who looked like he should have retired many years ago – short, fat of belly, bald, goggle-eyed and limping with rheumatics – a gallic Peter Lorre, hobbled from a waiting room. He introduced himself to Palethorpe, who handed him my papers. The gendarme glanced at the top sheet and immediately screamed, "*Arggh! Strasbourg! Merde, merde!*" and rolled his plump little eyes in mock horror. He and Palethorpe cross-checked the documents one last time, then the gendarme nodded to the prison guard, who emerged from his post with a bunch of keys.

This was it. I was getting out.

"Aldridge," someone yelled from across the courtyard.

I turned, half-expecting the Warden. But it was Dr Etienne.

The doctor grabbed my hand and pumped it. "Aldridge, I'm so glad I caught you. I wanted to say thank you for the beautiful painting you did of my wife. We both love it."

He handed me a new box of watercolours, with sable brushes and a metal water pot.

"My way of saying thank you," he said, handing me his business card. "If you get back to Paris, please look us up. We'd be happy to offer you our hospitality."

With a great rattle of keys, the guard opened the small door within the framework of the huge double gates and, following Palethorpe and the gendarme, I stepped through onto the sidewalk of a Paris street. It was one step that took me from insanity to sanity, from depravity to tranquillity. I considered kissing the cobblestones but decided not to. There were dollops of dogshit everywhere.

Palethorpe said a typically reserved British goodbye. We shook hands and he drove off in a beat-up Rover flying a Union Jack from its aerial. I stuffed my travel papers inside my suit and got into a black police Citroen beside the old gendarme. It shuddered into gear and we drove into the frenetic traffic in silence. I got the feeling the old gendarme was pissed at me, maybe because he had to escort me to Strasbourg, however far away that was.

"You stink," he said in perfect English, after we'd been driving ten minutes.

This was true. The faecal stench of prison permeated my hair, skin and clothes; it furred my tongue and coated my teeth. I could smell slop-out inside my nose and still feel the sting of carbolic acid in my eyes.

"Prejean's the name, Françoise Prejean," he said, offering me his chubby little pink hand to shake.

We shook.

"And yours is Aldridge, Alan," he continued. "Persona non grata of no fixed abode, soon to be a resident of Strasbourg in the Fourth Reich."

He said this in a good impression of Hitler. I figured he wasn't fond of Germans.

"We'll need to clean you up before presenting you at the border," he said. "The Germans love cleanliness before Godliness."

I agreed, but was already getting nervous this pot-bellied little man was about to propose we take a bath together.

"First, the *bain turc*," he said, slewing the car dangerously through traffic and entering a labyrinth of narrow alleys, halting outside a filthy-looking tenement. Above its peeling-paint front door was a sign written in gold lettering, TOMBOUCTOU BAIN TURC. We stepped from the summer cool of the alley through the doors into a brutal heat that instantly boiled sweat from every pore. An Arab greeted us with officious deference. Prejean peeled off some franc notes and paid the man.

"Monsieur Alan, this is Hamil," he told me. "He will escort you through the baths – and keep an eye on you. You will be here for approximately an hour. Across the street is Café du Caen, I'll be waiting for you there."

Hamil led me to a tiled cubicle. After I stripped, he helped me into a massive bathrobe, insisting on tying the belt personally.

I was leaking sweat; my pores felt like a colander.

Hamil took me through ornate Arabian Nights-type doors into a steam lounge. It was a purgatory of heat. My eyeballs boiled; it was painful to blink and painful not to. On ledges on every wall, fat men looking like beached whales lay naked, wheezing and gasping. Hamil advised that I remove my dressing gown and lie down on a shelf. I found a space, the wood slippery with steam. Hamil disappeared then, taking my suit, shirt, socks and shoes.

Being boiled alive, the heat overwhelmed me. I quickly succumbed to a deep sleep filled with fleeting images of Mesopotamia and flying carpets.

Hamil woke me when the time was up, and gestured that I should follow him. He helped me on with my bathrobe. I was feeling light-headed and faint. He led me through dark passageways, ornately decorated with flowered tiles in the Moorish style. The air turned chill as we entered a vaulted hall with a large pool, where more walrus-fleshed men wallowed in silence.

Hamil made jumping motions, encouraging me to get into the pool. I peeled off my bathrobe and noticed the inside was grey with dirt and grime, not just from La Santé but probably Bethnal Green, the Docks, all the way back to infant school as well.

I jumped into the water.

It was arctic, and gripped my body like a frozen glove. When I surfaced, Hamil stood at the poolside laughing, encouraging me to flap and circulate my arms. As I did so, a warm glow of well-being spread through me but my hour was ticking away. Hamil signalled me to get out. He helped me into a clean bathrobe, and together we hurried to my next venue, where I would experience torture by hot air.

Hamil led me along an underground tunnel into a small chamber. The place was empty. Set into the walls were two grills of ironwork bearing ornate Arabic inscriptions, and from each belched an agonising heat piped up from Hell itself, smelling of camphor and eucalyptus. Hamil indicated I had five minutes, and left me.

I lay on a shelf and let the stultifying hotness work its thermal sadism. My skin absorbed the herbal concoction even as it seared my lungs. I felt my heartbeat elevating dangerously, with the sudden loss of toxins from my body producing a giddy, hallucinatory experience that transported me back to the plains of China with Genghis Khan and his Mongol hordes.

Hamil returned and shook me back to reality.

We hurried on, to a new agony. In a vaulted room with heated floor tiles, men lay on straw mats like sun-seeking reptiles. Some were spread-eagled on tables, being mauled by subcutaneously endowed masseurs. Hamil directed me to get supine on a table. As soon as I lay on my stomach, fingers of steel kneaded and contorted my body, clasping my ankles and wrists, pulling them almost out of their sockets. Hands crawled all over me, stretching, squeezing bones and muscles as if I was a tube of toothpaste. At the end of the session I felt unglued and unhinged. It was as if every muscle, ligament, bone and particularly the spine had been disassembled and I'd never get put back the same again.

Next, soap sloshed over me. Now the hands, with amazing tenderness, worked the lather over my whole body, with scrupulous attention to my hands, feet and hair. Finally, buckets of cold water were poured over me, and I got rinsed down with big yellow sponges, then beckoned to stand by Hamil. He wrapped me in hot towels and escorted me to a dressing room, where my suit hung pressed. The rest of my clothes had been laundered and laid out with my prison-surplus shoes waxed and shiny as coal.

Exactly on the hour, Hamil said his au revoir. I then got ushered from the bathhouse. I crossed the street and went into the Café du Caen, where Gendarme Prejean sat at a table littered with the debris of what looked like an enormous meal: an empty terrine pot, gravy-smeared plates, half-empty quart bottle of wine, a ramekin crusted with leftover soufflé, a glass jar almost emptied of cornichons.

Prejean stood, greeted me and motioned that I should join him at the table. The café looked cheap and cheerfully working-class. Its only customers, apart from Prejean, were two butchers in blood-soaked overalls who stood at a small tin-topped bar, flirting with a tarty barmaid as she filled their glasses with beer from ornate spigots. I sat down opposite Prejean and immediately the barmaid came to the table, fluttering like some B-movie femme fatale.

"Madame Bouchard, may I introduce Alan Aldridge, persona non grata of the French Republic," announced Prejean grandly.

The butchers raised their glasses my way, and then laughed. Maybe being persona non grata wasn't such a bad thing after all.

Madame panted and cooed and smiled, pinching my cheek. She turned on her high heels and teetered quickly away, through beaded curtains. I'd met this type of barmaid before, coming on to customers so's she could milk them for a big tip. Within minutes, she returned and emptied a tray of baguettes, a slab of butter, a bowl of olive-y mush and an earthenware casserole containing two small chickens roasted to a golden brown, dotted with onions and mushrooms and coddled in a thick gravy. The dish exuded a pungent opulence of unguessable ingredients, far too sophisticated for my working-class nose, the gastronomic olfactory experience of which was limited to the odours of beef mince, fish and chips cooked in lard, jellied eels, bacon of course, and pickled onions.

Ravenous as a scrapyard dog, I plugged a chunk of bread into the gravy and ate it. After prison gruel and mush, the delicious complex tastes of the gravy sent my taste buds into a delirium. I tore off a chicken leg and literally slurped the buttery meat clean off the bone.

Prejean filled my glass with red wine and, raising his glass, offered a toast.

"To personas non gratas who gobble pigeons with glorious gusto."

He laughed and downed his wine but my glass stopped mid-air.

"Pigeon?" I barked, hurriedly extricating the leg bone from my mouth.

"Pigeon. Of course, Aldridge. What did you think you were eating, chicken?"

I immediately gagged as my throat tightened, then spasmed into vomit mode. My stomach heaved. For a second I thought I'd plant a pigeon pancake right there on the table. I hated pigeons. They were up there with bluebottles, fleas and rats on my list of God's most useless creations. Jesus, we English race pigeons but we definitely don't eat the flea-ridden, filthy, mangy things. I couldn't even think of them as birds, more like winged rats, scavengers of rubbish, guttersnipes of the avian world, gobble-gobbling in rubbish, dribbling shit wherever they congregated.

My pigeon phobia went back to when I was a kid. I found one dying, flopping about in the guttered rubbish of Wentworth Street Market. My first intention was to take the wounded bird home and nurse it until it could fly, but a stallholder warned me not to pick up the poxy thing, just to put it out of its misery, handing me an empty milk bottle and suggesting I bash the bird's pea-brain in, dispatching it to Pigeon Paradise. On my first nervous attempt at stoving its brains in, I missed. The bottle smashed on the pavement.

"Blimey, kid, you'll never get a job banging nails," quipped the stallholder. "Give it here," barked a yobbo selling neckties. "I'll wring its bleedin' neck."

"No, I'll leg it over to the RSPCA," I volunteered, grabbing the bird. I was surprised by its lightness, and hurried away before the subject of the pigeon's future became a major debate.

As it happened, the bird didn't have a future. It died a couple of minutes later, down Petticoat Lane. Feeling guilty,

I took the bird home intending to give it a royal burial in the grassless earth of our ten-foot-square back garden. I carried it into the kitchen, looking for a cereal box or a Tate & Lyle sugar bag for a coffin. When I laid the pigeon on the kitchen table, I remembered how, at school, I'd performed vivisection on a frog in biology class. I'd enjoyed the morbidity of poking around its insides. So I got the carving knife, always honed to Samurai sharpness by my father, so as to be able to carve the cheap, tough cut of meat we suffered through for Sunday lunch. I spread the bird's wings out and sliced its body from beak to backside. Blood spewed out as I put my fingers into the wound, broke the rib cage, and tore open the chest to lay bare the bird's innards.

At first I thought the pigeon had died from overeating vermicelli. Then, to my horror, I realised that millions of tiny threadworms boiled over every organ, thrashing in panic at their exposure to daylight. For a full five minutes I watched, repulsed yet fascinated, the ferment of the nematode legions – until, sickened, I shoved the writhing body into a paper bag and then dumped it over the fence into a dirty alley at the back of my house, knowing rats would make short work of the dead bird.

Back at the Café du Caen, Prejean appeared to have more on his agenda than simply escorting me to Strasbourg. The twat was smitten with Madame. Well into his second quart of cheap burgundy, alcohol had turned this pudgy little pudding of a person into a boisterous, if comical, Casanova, who lusted after the heavy-breasted Madame, beseeching her to enjoin him in undying love, kissing her neck, her cheeks, begging her on bended knees to spend the night together with him in an ecstasy of unending, passionate love-making. All his amorous protestations were being made much to the disturbance of the other customers, who were struggling to eat and drink between convulsions of laughter.

Prejean finally came to my table.

"It'sh time choogo," he slurred, dribbling wine and spittle down his uniform.

I stood. After Prejean kissed Madame for a considerable length of time – only coming up for air to whisper ludicrous endearments – we left the café and climbed into the Citroen. The streets were glassy with rain as Prejean drove like a Keystone Kop, weaving dangerously through the volatile Parisian traffic, violating stop signs and pedestrian crossings, slewing around corners until, miraculously, we braked to a jagged halt outside the ominous Gare du Nord.

At a ticket office on the station's main concourse, Prejean obtained my travel warrant for the journey to Strasbourg. We then stood at the Arrivée-Départ board, trying to decipher its numerical chaos while a loudspeaker system constantly blared out contradictory times and destinations. It was accompanied by insidious accordion muzak that giddied from every bar and café, even the lavatory.

"Platform eight," yelled Prejean and, pulling me by the wrist, he hurried me across the forecourt to the Strasbourg train.

We climbed aboard and joined the crush of people jamming the aisles.

"Aldridge," whispered Prejean in a confidential tone, leaning close, puffing his wino breath in my face. "The train ish nonshtop to Strasbourg. Here's your travel ID, your ticket, and persona non grata documentation, which you must present to the Deutsche Polizei Office at Strasbourg Bahnhof. Ask for Kaporal Fleish. I'll inform him by phone to expect you. Your ETA in Strasbourg is 3am."

"You're not escorting me?" I queried.

He chose to ignore my question. "Here's your financial entitlement from the prison authorities," he said. "And, a letter from Mr Palethorpe. He asked me to give it to you once you were on the train."

He fumbled two envelopes into my hands. I stuffed them into my suit pocket. On the platform a rail guard blew his whistle, then energetically waved a green flag. In response, the train engine belched its klaxon. A jolt shuddered through the carriages as the hydraulic brakes were released and, with a grinding of wheels on steel rails, the train clanked and hissed, flexing its power, slowly moving out of the station.

Panicked, Prejean quickly hugged me. "*Au revoir, Monsieur Aldridge.*"

Before I could respond, he turned and pushed his way along the crowded aisle. Through the window I saw him step from the train, stumble, fall over, stagger up and hobble back to the terminus.

It was an instant decision, one with no time for pre-meditation. One second I was heading to Germany, land of bratwürst and Büchenwald; the next, I was pushing my way between a bunch of French soldiers to the carriage door. With the train moving faster by the second, I opened the door and jumped, losing my balance, ending up sprawled on the platform. I watched as the train clattered northwards, until the haloes of its red taillights faded into the night.

Talk about impetuous.

Chaper Seven

As I stood up, a strange sense of euphoria buoyed through me. I realised I was free. I'd just stepped off the treadmill that had disciplined and methodically organised my whole life to date. For as long as I could remember, I'd been shunted from one regimen to another without any choice: Infant School, Cubs, Sunday Bible Class, Communion, Boy Scouts, Church (three times on Sundays), working on the docks. And then there were the endless chores at home: make the beds, wash up, take the rubbish out, polish the shoes, clean the knives and forks, each task performed with a parental accompaniment of "Hurry up, hurry up!" ringing in my ears constantly, like an obsession.

Now I had no chores, no shit to slop, no chickens to singe, no timecard to punch or bananas to schlep – nothing to stop me going south to Cannes and Jean the Gigolo. Nothing except my warped working-class conscience, brainwashed as I'd been since day one with the insidious philosophy that hard work and church were my only salvation. It was telling me to get back to London, face the music, quit fucking around in France, get back to the rat-race and my dead-end job down the docks. Work hard, get a girlfriend, put her up the spout, get married, move into a cardboard council flat, have kids. If you survive sixty fags a day, getting legless every weekend, with thirty years of staring moronically at the TV, you can retire fat and ugly with a pittance from the Docker's Union and end your days wearing incontinence nappies, muttering to yourself in the piss and vomit of an old people's home.

No thanks.

Ever since I was a kid I wanted to be an artist, to live a bohemian life like Toulouse-Lautrec – only with longer legs, wearing blue boots and velvet suits, sketching naked ladies by candlelight, painting in the manner of Gauguin and marrying a woman with one leg. As a school kid, whenever I mentioned my aspirations to be an artist to my parents they'd look aghast, like I'd owned up to having wet dreams over the Virgin Mary. "Artist!" my father would yell. "What d'you fink we are, the bleedin' Rothchilds? We can't afford to send you to art school. Waste of time. Get yerself a proper job. Artists! Bloody longhaired queers, the lot of 'em. If you ain't careful son, you'll end up like yer Uncle Sydney, dying of the pox and booze in a garret in Chelsea."

Sounded good to me. Uncle Sidney was the black sheep of the Aldridge family and only ever mentioned in the most hushed tones. Sidney had made his living drawing cartoons for *Punch*, a weekly satirical magazine famous for its illustrious contributors: Tenniel (illustrator of *Alice*), Heath Robinson, Henry Holiday, Aubrey Beardsley and Randolph Caldecott.

According to legend, in 1901 Uncle Sidney went on an assignment to the jungles of the Congo. He took with him a wind-up gramophone and a set of operatic arias by the world famous tenor, Enrico Caruso, which he played to the astonishment of a tribe there. They made him their king and he availed himself of the local ladies, some of them having genital diseases. When Sidney returned to England, it wasn't long before he felt like he was pissing barbed wire and he got delirious. He found out he had an exceedingly virulent form of syphilis. It proceeded to eat him up from balls to brain, so he turned to drink and died at the age of thirty, as my dad put it, "of pox and booze".

Even this tragedy had more allure than flogging one's guts out year after year for a measly weekly pay packet. So I chose Cannes. After all, I wasn't put on this planet simply to spend all my time being told what to do. I considered myself a rebel, an outsider. I coveted my isolation and transmuted my anger into poems and paintings. Full of cockiness, I swaggered back down the platform towards the main terminus.

My newly acquired self-assurance lasted but ten seconds. Ahead at the ticket barrier, a gaggle of gendarmes and railway officials stood in a group watching my approach, laughing and pointing at me. Shit. I felt like a rabbit caught in headlights. I must have been stupid to think my ship had finally come in, on a railway station. I knelt to tie my shoelace, anxious to gain my composure. Cops could smell fear a mile off. What I needed was a miracle – one where God's hand came down out of the clouds, picked me up and the next thing I'd know I'd be sitting on the beach at Cannes, downing a nice cold lager and surrounded by crumpet.

God was off-duty for miracles, though, and I started thinking about Albert 'the Bonce' Stephanidis instead. Albert, a Maltese somehow related to Tony the Greek, was to villainy what Einstein was to mathematics. Albert, who read Euclid and Plato, possessed a cunning and brilliant criminal mind. He was legendary for the nefarious schemes he conjured up to dispossess people, particularly the plummy-voiced and the smarmy, of their money.

Albert devised schemes to expand the Krays' protection racket; ran a lucrative abortion ring; pimped callgirls; and got the numbers on the gee-gees game. He had both sides of the fence covered, with judges; vice squad dicks; coppers – all of them on the take. Your average backstreet villain was in awe of him. Many thought he'd sold his soul to the Devil in return for earthly glory. So, one night in the Luciana, Tony tells me Albert the Bonce wants to see me, right away. This was like a royal command, so I legged over to Andy's Kebab House in Hackney to attend the great one. The place was packed, people wading into falafels, kebabs, molesting roast chicken, slurping up bowls of yogurt.

A waiter ushered me to a backroom. Albert sat at a small plastic table. He reminded me of King Farouk, plump, oily, with reptilian eyes and gold teeth. In one hand he nibbled at Turkish delight from a toothpick; in the other, he fastidiously sipped coffee from a tiny cup, his little finger extended. On that finger was a gold ring with a ruby the size of a testicle.

He ignored me for an appropriate length of time deemed necessary for a lowly gopher like me. At last he smiled, fluorescent light bouncing all over his teeth like they were pirate treasure.

"Aldridge, my dear," he said, welcoming me in a voice reminiscent of Alec Guinness as Fagin in David Lean's *Oliver Twist*. "Tony told me you are very artistic. Good, good. I have an urgent little job for you this weekend."

He pushed a camera and a portable flash across the table to me.

Albert explained that Robert Ryan and Rita Hayworth were "'aving it off on the side" and she happened to be married to a close friend of Albert's. The husband and wife were getting a divorce, and a photo of the wife with her paramour together would help the husband get a better financial settlement at the upcoming court proceedings. My mission was to get a photo of them drinking, screwing – whatever.

Ilford was a dump. Zero character. Just one big pile of worn-out, pre-war houses and a plastic high street where the most exciting night spot was the local Wimpy, spewing out its rancid stench. I got the electric from Stratford to Ilford and found The Cauliflower (courtesy of The A to Z Guide to London Albert lent me), where the couple often drank.

I bought myself a sherbet. With camera and flash concealed under my jacket, I cruised the public, then the saloon bar, but didn't see anyone fitting Albert's description: a bloke about six foot two, looking like Robert Ryan, the film star, an ex-paratrooper and a right evil bastard by all accounts. His bird was young, attractive, and looked like Rita Hayworth. I found the idea of a chick who looked like that famous actress, wandering around Ilford's pubs, very hard to believe.

I waited at the pub until closing time. The pair were a no-show, so I walked to a street nearby and Robert Ryan's bedsit. The neighbourhood stunk of decay and failure; it seeped from the endless rows of squalid, terraced, redbrick boxes. The only sign of life was the occasional TV glowing its blue light, illuminating dog shit and rubbish. Number 47 had no lights on. There were four push-buttons at the front door but no nameplates. I moved into the shadows of an alley that ran alongside the house, just in case the Old Bill came cruising by and sussed me for burglary. Only just in time, too, as headlights beamed onto the street and a Standard Vanguard slewed to a squeaky halt.

Two things. No-one who looks like Robert Ryan drives a dumb car like a Vanguard, and the driver was drunk. The couple got out of the car, laughing and definitely worse for drink. No doubt about it, he was a big bloke; in what little detail the wan streetlight revealed, he looked more like Winston Churchill. This threw me for a loop. Maybe these weren't the pair I was supposed to snap. She was pretty, but Rita Hayworth? Give me a break. She was a dead-ringer for Barbara Cartland, at least fifty. But then, maybe the low level of illumination in front of the house played tricks with her age.

As he fumbled for the key at the door, I considered stepping out of the shadows, banging off a couple of flashes and doing a runner. They were inside before I could put the plan into action, but she called the bloke Eric, and that's what Albert told me.

"Eric Hood, ex-paratrooper, a right bastard. So be careful. If he figures out what you're up to, he'll tear your head off."

No lights at the front of the house went on, so I cautiously made my way down the alley, which was as black as a burglar's pocket. I carefully threaded my way between tin dustbins. Just my luck, the top back-bedroom window showed a dull light, and briefly I saw Eric pulling a shirt over his head.

The only way up to the window would be by ladder.

I thought about calling it a day, coming back early the next morning and trying again, maybe catch them going to church. But the thought of getting the mission accomplished tonight and then handing the film over to Albert gave me enough incentive to go looking for a ladder. At the far end of the street I got lucky. In a window, I saw a hand-printed sign – Ronnie Hood, Windows Cleaned, Phone ILF 2001 – and, at the side of the house, I found a bicycle with two nine-foot ladders fixed alongside the crossbar. Ronnie would have to be seriously bow-legged to be able to ride the contraption; however, it was easy to wheel it out of the alley and along the street to 47. If a patrol car cruised the street now, I'd be bang to rights for burglary. I pushed the bike into the alley and managed to fumble the ladders against the back wall of the house, surprised at how awkward and heavy they were.

Now to check the camera and flash. I put it under my coat and pressed the button. White light exploded, totally screwing up my vision. All I could see now were two juddering white circles.

Somewhere close, a man started shouting.

I felt for the ladder, grabbing hold of its perpendicular sidepieces, blinking constantly to try and regain my vision, climbing upwards, rung by rung, until I reached the windowsill. My eyesight was good enough by now to see Barbara Cartland in bed, half-asleep. Winston Churchill, bollock-naked, was heading to the window. I ducked, but not quick enough. The window flew open outwards and hit me on top of the head, hard. For a second I thought I was a goner, expecting to fall backwards onto the concrete below, but I grabbed hold of the top rung, fumbling to get the camera one-handed out of my pocket.

I crouched just below the window. For a second, I thought it had started to rain. I was getting soaked. I looked up and, blow me down, stared right into Winston Churchill's one-eyed *wiener* taking an after-sex piss out of the window, the hot beer-loaded liquid splashing all over my head. What was even more remarkable was that he hadn't seen me. Dodging the stream, I started clicking the camera. The flash exploded two, three, four times, destroying my vision. I heard him scream, "What the fucking hell?" and banged off two more shots before I felt a huge hand close over my head – but my hair was wet, and he lost his grip. As blind as a bat, I stumbled down the ladder.

Barbara Cartland screamed.

Winston yelled, "I'm gonna fucking kill you!"

I believed him.

In the alley, I fell over Ronnie the Window Cleaner's bike, grabbed it in a panic and pushed it onto the street, jumped aboard and began pedalling furiously. Too furiously. The chain wasn't connecting with the gear wheel and I was just standing still. Finally, the chain bit, and I began to move slowly, though I was still blinded by two large, throbbing stars of pure white light, firmly nailed to my retinas. Now an animal scream, a baying of hyenas, a gurgling of blood ripped the silence of the street. I knew it was Winston, and pushed harder on the pedals. The growls, the laboured breath accompanied by a litany of curses, grew louder and closer. And closer! I turned out of fear. He was just a few feet behind and closing, naked, except for socks. I jumped from the bike and kept running. There was an horrific crash, an agonised scream as flesh and metal mangled together, followed by screeching.

"I'll kill you!"

I ran flat out all the way back to Ilford Station and caught the last train to Stratford, soaked and humiliated, but I got a laugh at the idea that Winston had bothered to put his socks on. Anyold how, the pictures turned out great. Albert's friend got his divorce and I earned a couple of quid for my trouble.

Back in my current predicament in France and standing on the train platform, I wondered why the hell I was thinking about Albert the Bonce. Then it came to me. One night over at Andy's, Albert talked about a weekly little scam he and his friend Anistasias, a cab driver, pulled off. Dressed to the nines, they'd take the cab up West, either Soho or Kensington, find an expensive Italian restaurant. Albert knew his way round an Italian menu, never Indian or Chinese. They would enter independently and get separate tables. Albert would order prosciutto with Parma ham, antipasto of anchovies and salamis, washed down with a chilled Pinot Grigio. Main course would always be steak, a green salad, a plate of pasta and, if possible, a bottle of Brunello di Montalcino – red as ox blood, strong and fruity, pricey too. Dessert was a tiramisu, Havana cigar, and several glasses of grappa.

Across the room, Anistasias had done the business too, running up an exorbitant bill. Now was the time for Albert's dramatic performance. He filled his mouth with tiramisu, gargled, screamed, clutched his heart, then toppled off the chair and laid on the carpet, his eyes bulging, gasping, slobbering tiramisu all over the place. The waiters, the maître d', they stood transfixed with horror. Fat Albert heaved pitifully, blowing snot from his nose, frothing spumoni. As waiters gathered, readying to carry Albert to the bathroom, Anistasias strode over, knelt and felt Albert's pulse.

"This man is having an epileptic seizure," he declared. "I'm a doctor. Please help me get him to my car. I'll drive him to a hospital. He needs urgent medical attention."

The waiters, only too happy to get rid of the embarrassment, carried the convulsing Albert outside to the parked car. Anistasias would thank them, then drove off back to Hackney with two expensive bills sitting unpaid back at the restaurant. So, was God telling me to pull an epileptic fit in front of the cops? Frankly, I didn't have the bottle.

Sometimes doing the obvious saves a lot of aggravation. I simply walked through the barrier and held up my wrist, as though looking at an imaginary watch, tapping it with my finger. I shrugged my shoulders with exaggerated Gallic gestures, indicating that I'd just missed my train. It worked. The guards and police laughed. I quickened my pace and passed the barrier, glad to reach the crowded concourse. Now to check the envelopes. The first contained an officious-looking letter on prison paper, a note from Dr Etienne with a one hundred franc note.

I threw the letter away.

The second held two hundred francs with Best Wishes and a cheeky IOU from Palethorpe, with his Paris address. I felt rich but wasn't sure, then I remembered: way back at Orly, I'd exchanged ten pounds for sixty francs, so I reckoned I had approximately fifty quid. I was rich.

I followed Metro signs down dirty stairwells and found a ubiquitous map of the Metro stations, fingered Gare du Nord and searched for... Was it Gare du Sud to Cannes? I didn't find a station of that name or anything close, so I asked passers-by but either they didn't understand, didn't want to, or were in too much of a hurry. Maybe, with my beatnik hair and sackcloth suit, I looked too weird.

I gave up and went to the ticket office. Remembering my last experience at Orly, I didn't have much faith in being treated civilly, but got in line anyway.

"*Parlez-vous anglais?*" I asked politely when I got to the ticket window.

"*Non,*" said the ticket clerk, in a voice full of apathetic disdain.

I put my one hundred franc note on the counter.

"*Billet pour Cannes, um, la Gare du Cannes.*"

The ticket clerk, looking totally perplexed, waved me away from the window and yelled "*Au suivant.*"

"FUCK!" exploded out of me as a way to vent my frustration. I stuck my money back in my jacket pocket. But luckily, English, as opposed to say, Afghani, is more than any other an international language, and so a man who looked Turkish and had the sleepy eyes of Victor Mature approached me.

"Fuck, I understand," he said. "I am here as a poor man to help you."

He smiled and had perfect teeth. He took hold of my arms in a brotherly way, pulling me disconcertingly close. I could smell Balkan smells on him: strong tobacco, stale yogurt, kebab smoke, mastika.

"Confide in me entirely your problem," he whispered, with intimidating politeness.

"I need to get to Cannes by train."

Before the Turk could answer, a thin man with sallow eyes and a walrus moustache pushed rudely between us, not stopping to apologise, hurrying away in a half-run, half-walk to an escalator.

Rude son of a bitch.

"Cannes. You need Gare de Lyon. Change trains at Châtelet," the Turk informed me.

God, Châtelet... It seemed a lifetime ago since I struggled out of that crowded station to stroll the Rue Saint-Denis and take a ride with Madame Pom Pom. I thanked the Turk, who bowed obsequiously and ambled towards the escalator. I got in line, confident in my ability to purchase a ticket to the correct location using French, and practiced the sentence, "*Gare de Lyon, s'il vous plaît*", over and over until I reached the booth.

"*Gare de Lyon, s'il vous plaît,*" I said with total confidence.

The clerk laid a ticket on the counter as I reached into my coat pocket for the one hundred note.

There was no note. No crinkle of currency. Nothing.

In disbelief, my fingers anxiously spidered around the pocket. It was still empty, yet I clearly remembered putting the one hundred bill in there after my first encounter with the ticket clerk.

"*Au suivant!*" yelled the clerk again, waving at me to step aside from the booth.

At one of the ticket-vending machines nearby, an old man stood begging. Yellow-skinned and cadaverous, he appeared to be dying of cirrhosis or some other fatal ailment of the liver. His moth-eaten suit and cardboard-box shoes completed the impression that he'd escaped from a death camp such as Auschwitz.

He caught my eye and laughed a toothless laugh at my quandary. Then, with theatrical gestures, he dipped his hand in his pocket and, pulling it out, rubbed his thumb and fingers together in the age-old signal for gelt, money, his eyes wide with greed.

The penny dropped. I'd been robbed – pickpocketed by the cunning fat Turkish bastard with the perfect teeth. And no wonder they were perfect. He could probably afford the best dentist in Paris. No doubt he dipped the money when he pulled me close, then palmed it off to Walrus Moustache. Panicked, I felt in my trouser pocket. Happily, my fingers closed over the other two hundred franc notes. Holding them tightly, I got in line.

Third time lucky, I purchased a ticket to Gare de Lyon.

The train, Côte D'Azur Express, a red-eye, rumbled promptly out of the Gare de Lyon at 11:30pm. I had to sprint to catch it, just managing to yank open the door of the last carriage; but, as I tried to jump in, a man dressed in a black habit and skull cap fell out backwards, into my arms. He must have been leaning against the door. With the train muscling faster and the platform rapidly running out, I held tightly to the door and a handrail on the carriage, cradling the screaming novitiate, struggling to get aboard as the train's speed twisted my legs to taffy. Falling to my death beneath the wheels became a real possibility. Fortunately, with the help of the passengers on board, we got hauled to safety. Only just in time, as the flapping door smacked into a no-entry barrier at the end of the platform. It slammed shut with a thundering crash!

The train was packed. The aisles and every wooden seat of the third-class compartment were a veritable insectarium of human activity, nothing like the dour and sullen crowd on the Strasbourg train. Here was more a carnival, a Moroccan bazaar. There was a rowdy chaos of hollering and shouting in languages far from France: Zanzibar and Tanzania, Tunisia and the Cameroons.

Moving among the crowd, a Greek with a greying, frizzled beard hawked miniature bottles of cheap brandy. A Vietnamese woman tried to sell strips of cardboard-looking flesh that smelled of rotten fish, pushing her way through beery Germans flirting with clumsy, lipsticked office girls in summery dresses. An Arab, charlatanism blazing in his eyes, hustled cigarettes hand-rolled with rough-cut Egyptian tobacco from a tiny machine. Another sold bags of dates.

Working-class families huddled together. The wives and kids bedded down on the floor using duffel bags and knapsacks as pillows, while the husbands played a game of whist. Each player, after much windmilling of the arms, smashed down his card. This caused a whirlwind of shouts from the other players.

Woven among the carriage's hubbub came gusts of Arabic music and transistorised rock 'n' roll. I got sandwiched between a corpulent woman who looked to be from the same gene pool as the Michelin Man, and the novice priest, who was still whimpering after his fall from grace and near-death experience. The three of us were pressed indecently together, our bodies swaying to and fro in unison with the movements of the train as it hurtled south. Beyond the windows I could see the glow-worm flash of traffic on motorways; looming factories made eerie by sodium light; industrial wastelands and endless suburbia until nothing but blackness, dotted by a mango-coloured moon and the occasional signal light that streaked by like a comet.

Clankety-clank. Clankety-clank.

Awakened by the familiar noise of the prison guards' rise and shine signal, I blinked dozily, half-expecting to be back in La Santé. Instead, I was standing tightly wedged among a throng of passengers, as the train shuddered to a clanking halt. Immediately the carriage doors flew open and I got swept from the train onto the platform by the surging exodus of excited travellers, anxious to begin their vacations, swarming towards the ticket barrier like an unstoppable flow of lava.

I'd arrived in Cannes.

The sweltering humidity and noise inside the station reminded me of the parrot house at London Zoo. The early morning air had already ovened to over 90°F (32°C), and the bedlam was dizzying. There was the growling of diesel engines shunting; police sirens and porters' whistles as they squabbled over luggage; and the hundreds of passengers who were pushing, shoving, jostling, grunting, some staggering drunkenly. There were lost kids yowling for their mummies; tired kids doing tantrums. The news vendors were yelling out their morning editions to the accompaniment of the sonorous klaxons of trains arriving or leaving.

I hunkered down in the stampeding crowd, anxious not to attract the attention of the local gendarmes. I needn't have worried; there were no cops at the gate. Once past the ticket collector, I hurried across the forecourt into the Gents. Entering, I did a double take. Surely I'd made a mistake? Where was the acrid stench of piss and excrement, bothersome flies, shit-smeared cubicles, pornographic graffiti, scrawled telephone numbers offering buggery, hand-jobs and blowjobs? Where were the names and numbers of wives deemed dirty sluts? Where was the trough swilling with cloudy yellow liquid, clogged with cigarette butts, half-chewed sandwiches and newspaper?

This john was spotless. It even had toilet paper in the stalls.

My purpose now was to get rid of my travel warrant, my persona non grata papers and any other *papiers* that would be incriminating if the police stopped me. I figured that from now on, I'd say I had my passport stolen, and take my chances. I went into a cubicle and locked the door, pulled out the *papiers*, tore them up, dropped them in the pan and pushed the flush button. Nothing happened. Then I heard a scuffle in the next cubicle and smelled a very strong cologne – gardenia. I heard someone humming Onward Christian Soldiers. I looked under the partition and saw a pair of brown brogues. They were facing the wrong way for someone having a crap. Panicked, thinking it might be a copper, I opened the door in a hurry and ran to the station's main entrance.

Outside, the sun blazed in a sky of purest blue. More importantly, there were palm trees everywhere. To me, palm trees represented romance, intrigue and adventure. Until then, the closest I'd ever got to a palm tree was the movies, the trademark on a bar of Palm Toffee, and folding palm leaves into crosses at Sunday School on Palm Sunday. The palms, gilded by the morning sun, hovered like enormous spiders over the entrance to the station, where cab drivers shouted prices and destinations at potential customers. Hotel buses stood in line surrounded by a confusion of tourists, who were being pestered by gypsy-women selling bunches of lavender, and pedlars pushing postcard souvenirs.

I had two first orders of the day. One: to get rid of my prison-issue suit. Even though I'd got the jacket folded under my arm, the trousers were torture, like wearing a pair of itchy ovens. Two: breakfast. A plate of fried eggs, bacon, fried bread and a cup of tea. That would go down nicely.

I strode off along Rue Venizelos in search of breakfast and a pair of cotton pants. There were no shortage of cafés, but these weren't your doorstop-and-dripping cafés of East London, stunk up with burnt grease and Woodbine smoke. No, these were all posh, with mirrors and brass. They had potted plants and urns filled with roses, for crissake. Like Paris, the cafés had tables out front, overflowing with customers – svelte women in toque hats and pearl chokers talking anxiously among themselves; businessmen cramming *Le Soir*; prosperous matrons clutching crocodile handbags and poodles; tourists ogling girls looking like mannequins with their ponytails, skin-tight leotards and bra-less T-shirts. The girls were flirting with youths, tanned and romantic-looking, in tattered jeans and colourful shirts. Everyone sipped coffee between gesticulated conversation. They nibbled on croissants to the accompaniment of radios emitting a medley of waltzes, polkas, ballads and pop tunes.

They were all too poncey-percy for me. Anyway, each place looked intimidatingly expensive and, when I'd stop to check a menu, a surly waiter would give me a 'Don't you dare come in here, you scruffy bastard' evil-eye look.

I ducked down a narrow alley, quiet as a church after the hubbub of the main street. The shops here were tiny, quaint, cowered in perpetual shadow. I found a run-down clothes store, a *magasin d'habillement*, its façade of peeling blue paint embellished with gold-painted words: *tailleurs, pantalons, bretelles, chemises, imperméables…* The small window of the shop was a masterpiece of accidental surrealism, with a headless tailor's dummy wearing a blue work shirt, on top of which the owners had set a potted geranium plant wearing a beret. The effect was bizarre.

I went inside.

Chapter Eight

The shop was empty, a mournful greyness enveloping the whole place. Glass counters showed off detached collars of every imaginable shape and size with collar studs, leather gloves, berets, braces and underwear. On shelves, work shirts and trousers were neatly stacked. At the end of the counter stood the cash register, next to it a birdcage with tomtits and chaffinches, so immobile they had to be stuffed. The till seemed to smile invitingly at me. It would take no time at all to open the drawer, grab the money and be outside on the street before you could say Jack Robinson. I'd done it before, many times, particularly at a cake shop called The Tryst, run by a pair of old hooves. But then there would be two of us conspirators. My mate Geoff, he would sidetrack the owner, Lionel, to the front window, to point out a rock cake, wanting to know the price. While Lionel's back was turned, I'd ease open the till, lift out as many fivers and pound notes as I could in a couple of seconds, and then we'd have money for ciggies and the movies.

As I moved round the counter and stood behind the cash register, the birds went into a paroxysm of screeching, beating each other frantically with their wings in a violent skirmish, clawing and pecking, thrashing against the cage. Out of nowhere appeared a gnomish old man with pince-nez and a nicotine-stained beard. Blow me down if the little birds weren't the old geezer's security alarm. I felt a right twat, caught standing behind the counter with my sticky fingers almost in the till.

"What d'you want?" asked the gnome curtly, eyeing me up and down suspiciously, as if guessing my intentions to steal money from the till.

Rather than garble my needs in fractured French, I pointed to the denim work shirts and jeans.

"D'you have money?" he asked, moving to the doorway, perhaps thinking I might grab what I needed and do a runner.

The question pissed me off. What did I look like? A dosser, a down-and-out? I contemplated laying a knuckle sandwich right in his moosh but decided against it.

I flashed my hundred-franc note.

"What prison are you from?" he inquired.

Jesus, the little gnome not only taught little birdies to be burglar alarms, I thought. He's also psychic.

"What?" I countered, avoiding the question.

"Marseilles, Paris, which one?" he persisted.

"What's it to you?" I countered.

"Your suit, it's a dead giveaway. Prison issue. Only an idiot would be walking around Cannes wearing it. The cops here like to keep the town clean and tidy for the tourists. They don't like ex-cons. They could pick you up on suspicion the second they see you, keep you locked up indefinitely."

I didn't see the point of beating round the bush any further. "Santé," I said.

It was as if the word had a magical allure, for the old gent's face exploded into a wide, toothsome smile.

"Ah, the crown jewel in our penal system," he cooed. "Congratulations. That's a tough joint. Relax, son. I'm an ex-con myself. Eugène Artois is the name."

He grabbed my hand and shook it forcefully.

"Santé..." He said the word with a tone of reverence, like it held the power of a prayer. "You must have come across Duc El Baraka? Nice kid from Lyon, doing a ten stretch for counterfeiting."

"Duc El Baraka's a hairy lunatic of a gorilla from Algiers, doing life for murder," I corrected, then related my own personal dramas with le Duc.

Little Eugène smiled, convinced of my genuineness. He pulled a dark-blue denim work shirt and a pair of white, French-made jeans, handing them to me. "Take these," he said. "On the house, kid. Get changed and I'll dump your suit. If you need a place to crash or get in a jam, give me a call anytime, day or night."

He handed me a business card. I got changed. There was nothing else to do but thank him, have breakfast, and move on to the Carlton. Eugène and I shook hands.

I stepped out into the alley feeling I was part of a criminal fraternity.

The alley opened into a busy market. It was an Aladdin's cave of edible delights, filled with the murky scents of melons, pears and the conflicting smells of cloves and sweet basil. Each stall contained miracles of food: baskets of mushrooms, garlics, and precarious mountains of tomatoes. There was a charcuterie that had sausages, dishes of pâté, towering monoliths of lardy meat, and a veritable zoo of furry and feathered creatures hanging, glassy-eyed, from hooks.

Then I caught scent of a buttery smell: a whiff of freshly baked bread that enticed me to find its source. I discovered a small bakery. Inside, its counters were stacked with baskets loaded with croissants – some plain, others stuffed with chocolate, olives, raisins and various cheeses. Coffee, smelling strong and exotic, percolated in glass jars on top of an old-fashioned oven.

I bought a couple of plain croissants, still hot and mushy, ungreasy yet aching of butter. They were perfectly complemented by a cup of coffee that, unlike the thin and powdery stuff I slurped in London, was thick, earthy and deliciously sweet. Seated at a table in the window, I luxuriated in the fact that I had nothing better to do than to enjoy the moment. I sat back and watched the market crowd.

Dealers, exporters, buyers and wholesalers were standing around in groups, smoking and chatting, discussing produce prices, while tourists swarmed frenetically from stall to stall, with a determination and ingenuity to get rid of their money as quickly as possible. Suddenly I got this overwhelming feeling of someone clocking me. I turned from the window to survey the café and locked eyes with an evil-looking bastard: a middle-eastern thug, crumpily dressed, replete with a vicious scar down one cheek. He had the cold, pitiless eyes of a hyena viewing prey. With me the prey.

He smiled, stood and oiled over to my table, sitting himself down.

"Alan Aldridge. Nice to meet you."

His accent sounded like he had a throat full of sand. I didn't respond, flabbergasted that he knew my name. Was he an undercover cop?

Let him do the talking, I thought. It's his card game and he's holding all the aces.

"Alan Aldridge," he repeated. "Persona non grata."

The words hit me like a sledgehammer.

A feeling of dread and nausea spidered through me. Suddenly, my Cannes fun-in-the-sun enterprise seemed in jeopardy. I leaned forward to rest my head in my hands, feeling the cold sweat beading on my forehead.

I noticed his shoes. They were brown brogues. His sickly cologne, gardenia, wafted into my face. No self-respecting cop would wear gardenia but a wimp, pimp, or cheap crook? Maybe. And what was he doing, slumming round a station lavatory? A psycho peeper out for cheap thrills? The creep must have fished out the torn pieces of my *papiers* from the pan, figured out I was illegal, now he was gonna finger me. For what? Money. I'd got about a hundred and forty francs. So, any second, the scumbag was going to ask for dough in return for not turning me in to the cops. Blimey, I thought. I have to admire his fortitude to make a few bob. Cool, so I'll be broke but only momentarily. Once I get to the Carlton, Jean will lend me cash. Then a nasty idea hit me, one that fuelled my burgeoning anxiety. What if Jean isn't in Cannes? But right now, I'm more concerned with the surly-looking bloke across the table. What's his little game?

I drank my coffee and waited. He stared at me, unblinking, his eyes blank and glassy like a dead fish. Junkie's eyes...

The guy's an addict, a dealer. Don't tell me he's setting me up to do a dope deal.

I was wrong on all counts. Hyena pulled a wallet from his pocket, flipped it open and flashed a police badge and photo ID. He then leaned closer, his voice dropping to a rasp.

"Don't give me any trouble, Roast Beef," he said. "Or I'll separate your head from your arsehole. Put your right arm on the table."

My mouth went dry and bile surged up in my throat. On the street, people were enjoying themselves milling around stalls, spending money. With his powerful build and bull neck, I didn't argue. He niftily snapped a handcuff on my wrist, clamping the second bracelet to his own wrist.

"Okay, you dumb bastard," he growled. "Let's go."

We stood. I trailed behind him out onto the street, sick to my stomach.

We walked downhill, along a narrow street thronged with people, emerging through an arched stone gateway onto a quay harbouring a gaggle of colourful, painted fishing boats bobbing up and down like feeding geese. Their reflections were liquefying into fragments of stained glass on the trembling water. Beyond the harbour wall lay the Mediterranean: a broad swipe of cerulean blue, scintillated gold by the sun and scarred with the criss-cross wake of tugs and speedboats. To the west, the geometric jumble of Cannes and its beaches quivered behind a veil of heat.

Along the Quai Saint-Pierre, the atmosphere was hot and horny. Raucous music blared everywhere. Jukeboxes and radios mish-mashed the latest American pop music with the grind of street barrel organs and the wheeze of accordions. The humid air, thick as honey, reeked of suntan oil and the scent of sex. Flesh and skin paraded past me in an endless jungle of tits and arse. There were breasts the size of melons. Peek-a-boobs. There were jiggling buttocks, and bellies bangled by fat. Bronzed thighs and legs went up forever, from high heels and chained ankles, to end at g-strings barely adequate in covering a woman's garden of delights. It was diableedinbolical that here I was, in this steamy paradise, and I couldn't stop, have a ciggie and check out the birds.

Mr Hyena pulled me along at ten steps to the dozen – anxious, no doubt, to get me booked and behind bars so he could get back to his beat, sneaking around the Gents toilet at Cannes Station. He suddenly veered up an alley, cool and shadowed after the blinding heat of the quay. It was quiet too, with none of the noisy mill of people. We strode past a chemist and a fruit shop, where baskets spilled onto the pavement, full of swollen Morello cherries and apricots that smelled of summer.

Next, he yanked me through a doorway and we were standing in a bar, a room of shadows, the low light baffled by red silk shades. It looked like a Soho clip joint, with mirrors everywhere – walls, ceiling – adding bizarre reflections. It was like some place out of an Orson Welles movie. Seated at the bar were three or four girls in short skirts and high heels, listening to a couple of drunken French sailors mouth off about life on the ocean waves.

At the far end sat four ugly-looking leather boys with shaved heads and jack-boots, playing dice. I knew the type, well into S&M, getting tanked early, looking forward to a day of violence. The barman had elephantitis, his gut big as a watermelon. Nice crowd.

Mr Hyena got two brandies. It was 10:30am. Events were turning dangerous. I'm handcuffed to a cop whose motives are highly questionable – a big geezer, weighing in at a flabby 250lbs, who's got macho tattoos on his arms but talks like a mincer. A dangerous mix.

Hyena jabbed me hard in the ribs with his pointed elbow. "Drink," he demanded. "*Salud.*"

He slung his brandy down his throat, and then watched me with those dead eyes. I'm no spirits drinker but, to keep the peace, I drank the brandy and let most of it dribble down my chin. What little I did swallow, it peeled the membrane from the back of my throat and set my mouth on fire. I coughed and sputtered. The patrons laughed, shouting out stuff like "*mon pauvre bébe, petite fée*" – nothing complimentary, I'm sure.

One of the women, wearing a dress like a second skin, came over and gave me a glass of water. I *merci beaucoup*-ed her. She moved very close, fluttering her false eyelashes and pouting her lips provocatively. She stroked my shirt and then moved lower, but Hyena pushed her angrily away. She backed off and it was then I noticed she had morning stubble. She was a he, a transvestite.

Hyena pulled me across the room to a glass-windowed telephone kiosk. He stepped inside and jerked the folding door closed, trapping the chain of the cuffs and me outside. I noticed a pool table at the back of the room. It had no pockets. This whole place was a fuck-up.

Hyena got talking on the phone. This, maybe, was a slim chance to escape. If I could pull my hand out of the bracelet, I'd be out on the street doin' a runner, long before the big bastard could struggle out of the kiosk. I gripped the cuff in my left hand, bunched the fingers of my right as tight as I could and then pulled and pulled, until the metal bit deep into the back of my hand, tearing off strips of skin and opening bloody cuts.

There was no way I'd get the handcuff off. Whoever invented them knew what they were doing. I guess that was the whole point of the damn thing. I'd read that foxes, wolves, even dogs would gnaw through their own leg to get free of a trap. I had such an overwhelming feeling of dread about Hyena and his motives, I was prepared to give it a try but then, one of the girls strutted over to me. She pressed a hair clip into my hand and whispered in a Scouse accent, "Better watch your pretty little —"

She got no further. Hyena burst out of the kiosk, screaming at her. The two of them went at each other verbally, until the barman shouted at them to shut up, and the Scouser returned to the bar. Hyena pulled me to a table. We sat and he demanded two more brandies. I'd been in a lot of iffy situations and always managed to talk myself out, like this one time, I got myself caught by a rival gang at the back of the Hammersmith Palais. They were set to give me a good kickin' into next week. I told them I couldn't give a fuck whatever they did, I'd still get to Hammersmith Hospital even if I had to crawl, as my mum only had hours to live, dying of cancer. Well, the prats all backed off – except a ginger kid called Red, who punched me in the mouth, told me I was a lippy bastard and to get going.

Of course my mum wasn't ill, but it was a nice creative line off the top of my head, and got me out of a right seeing-to.

With Hyena, though, this wasn't an option. The barman, who looked about as happy as a Jehovah's Witness without a copy of *Awake*, waddled to our table. Balancing a tray with two brandies on his enormous belly, he banged down the glasses and muttered French swear words, *merdes* mixed with spittle. Hyena retaliated in Algerian. I got the distinct feeling Hyena wasn't welcome in this red-lit den of iniquity. Giddy with drink, the Liverpudlian lass struggled off her barstool and, in a tarty impersonation of Marilyn Monroe at her sexiest, navigated unsteadily between tables, her backside jelly-rolling. She parted her ruby lips, licking around them lasciviously. As she passed our table, she blew Hyena a kiss. He snarled and almost tore my arm out of its socket when he tried to backhand her with his handcuffed arm.

She leaned over and whispered in my ear. "Help is nigh, ducks."

Hyena stood threateningly. He swore at her as she tottered into the kiosk, closed the door and made a call. Hyena became increasingly agitated. He slugged down his brandy and told me to drink up, that the police would be here soon to drive us to headquarters where charges would be filed against me.

Events beyond my understanding now unravelled thick and fast. Liverpool finished her call. She slunk her sexy carriage back to her barstool. It was hard to believe she was a man. The phone rang in the kiosk. Hyena was up and running at the first ring, pulling me arse-over-tit off my chair as he grabbed the phone. He listened, doing a lot of nodding and guttural *ouis*. When he finished the call, we sat back at the table. He watched the door anxiously. A French sailor somehow managed to bump and bounce his way to the jukebox and fired up some rock 'n' roll.

Through the front entrance, stepping in from the brightness of the street, came two gendarmes. My heart sank. Here's my escort back to jail, I thought but, as always on this voyage, the unexpected happened. Hyena stood, I thought to greet the cops and hand me over. Instead, he pushed the table violently to one side, keyed open his handcuff, and did a runner out through the rear exit of the bar. The gendarmes gave chase. I could only stand and watch the whole event, handcuffs dangling from my wrist, comprehending nothing.

Liverpool beckoned me to the bar.

"You better make yourself scarce, cutie," she said. "That nasty bastard you were with, he was a *bardash*, a well-known pimp. Deals in pretty boys. Who knows what he had lined up for you? A fag party on a yacht? You could've been on your way to a male brothel in Algeria. He's into the white-boy slave trade. You better scarper." She turned to Watermelon. "Get these cuffs off the poor sod."

The barman pulled out a bunch of keys, screws and nails from behind the bar. With a minimum of fuss, he had me free.

"Come back tonight, dear," said Liverpool. "And 'ave some fun. Right now, I'd make yourself scarce in case the cops come back."

I exited, right quick. A black Merc cruised to a halt outside the bar as I stepped out onto the street. I ducked into the entrance of the fruit shop and watched, as a pair of Algerians got out of the car and hurried into the bar. I had no doubt they were Hyena's accomplices, come to take delivery of me. I ran, not slowing until I merged with the crowd swilling along

Quai Saint-Pierre. I got directions to the Carlton and, buoyed by the thought I would soon be drinking an ice-cold beer with Jean, joined the streams of tourists promenading the Croisette, the main drag of Cannes. The beach was on one side, where parasols of every stripe shaded near-naked sun-worshippers, and on the other, luxury hotels, boutiques and expensive restaurants.

The Carlton took me by surprise. It was enormous – a gigantic wedding cake, ornately confectioned. Nothing less than Buckingham Palace-by-the-Sea. The only hotels I'd ever stayed in had been pokey little dumps, known in the theatre business as digs, usually one-up one-down converted terraces vulgarly painted pink or mauve, with ludicrous names like Shangri-la Hotel or, worse, Denrose, Bobjane, Ednabill, or any other combination of the owners' first names.

Digs consisted of two, three bedrooms at most; some had beds but those that served as short-term lodging houses for the theatrical profession had bunk beds. The bathroom was communal. Baths were obtained by putting a shilling in a meter. This would provide about eight inches of lukewarm water. The lavatory would often be outside in the back garden. Breakfast was the only meal served, 6:30am to 7:30am. It consisted of coffee made from granules, tea, burnt toast, margarine and cornflakes.

The landlady ruled the roost in these pathetic excuses for hotels. They were usually spinsters one and all, dowdy old ladies who got sadistic delight in locking the front door at precisely 10:15pm, fifteen minutes before the pubs closed. Of course, no self-respecting Englishman would leave a pub before closing. This meant the lodgers got up to all kinds of shenanigans to gain entry, from picking locks to leaving windows open. But the boys of The Queens Repertory Company, an all-male troupe of amateur thespians, quickly learned the best bet was to send an envoy back to the digs at ten and, if possible, he'd get drinking a nightcap with the landlady, whisky with a sedative.

As a last resort there was always chloroform...

As a kid I never went to the seaside on holiday. My mum couldn't afford it, so my first experience of a hotel was digs. Out of work, I managed to land a summer job as a tea boy slash assistant to the stage assistant of Queens, which was managed by Raymond, who owned a furniture shop in Leyton and daydreamed of screwing Ricky Nelson. His mum knew my mum, and that's how I got the gig. Of course, my mum thought Raymond was such a nice man and hadn't a clue he was as bent as a two-bob watch. The company was putting on Sandy Wilson's *Boyfriend* in drag, a bold venture considering the show's tour was booked to play in working men's clubs and a few flea-bit theatres throughout the industrial wastelands of the north of England, from Barnsley to Bradford.

Queens was an apt name for the troupe. I quickly learned the play was no more than an excuse for this bunch of perverts, drug addicts and alcoholics to leave the repression of London to go on a rampage up north, boozing and buggering. The twenty actors packed their suitcases with poppers (amyl nitrate); mogadons (depressants); Spanish fly (aphrodisiac); purganol (laxative); Mentholatum Cough Syrup (contained ether); Eno's Fruit Salts (effervescent saline); cocaine (hidden in a powdered-sugar box); and hashish. They took bags of marijuana along with morphine; sleeping pills; boxes of surgical gloves; truncheons; strings of plastic beads; black leather masks; jock straps borrowed from Stratford YMCA cricket team (and very smelly); frogman outfits; enemas; dildoes (electric and manual); jars of Vaseline; and horse tranquillisers. Then there was a variety of chains, cords, handcuffs, thumbscrews, nipple clamps, a camera and flash (to record their various gang-bangs) and an array of Swedish gay porn books.

They climbed aboard the rented coach at Stratford and headed north up the M1. It was the beginning of a six-week orgy of every known perversion, and some about to be invented. The tour came to a screeching halt in Halifax. The show at the town hall had gone down well, a packed house. The English, particularly provincials, love drag. After the curtain, the Queens vaudevillians, still in greasepaint, rushed to the public bar of the Crown, anxious to down as much booze as possible in the half an hour left until closing time. They hoped to pick up some rough trade: working-class youths. As always, I bought myself half a bitter and skulked into a dark corner to watch the drama unfold.

Raymond, AKA Rachel to the troupe, quickly worked the room, chatting up local lads and buying them double brandies; salt-and-vinegar crisps; even splashing out for the occasional pig's trotter or pickled onions – anything to get them amenable and pissed. The youths – mostly labourers, factory workers, young toughs – weren't fooled by Ray's largesse. They saw right through his bullshit but were quite happy to freeload off an old queen. I'd listen to them plotting to kick the shit out of the whole bunch of what they called southern bum-bandits, nicking their wallets, trousers and underpants once they got onto the streets after closing time. But once Ray chose his prey, they were doomed, as sure as the fly in the spider's web and the fish in the jaws of the shark. Their drinks were mickey-finned: laced with a pharmaceutical concoction perfected over the years to make the victims docile, woolly-brained, yet willing to fornicate with their own long-dead great-grandmother.

Back at the digs in Halifax, Mrs Cooper, the landlady, slept like a log in front of the TV. The screen was a snowy blizzard of white noise, the BBC having long since closed down for the night. She thought her new guest Raymond a nice man. He'd bought her a bottle of her favourite tipple, Port, so she could enjoy a sip while watching *Come Dancing*. The port contained a cocktail of tranquilisers, although Raymond had miscalculated the dosage. Mrs Cooper would sleep almost flat-lined for thirty-eight hours straight.

When the actors got back, they lifted the snoring Mrs Cooper up to her bedroom, and then set about turning the front room into a den of debauchery. The heavy curtains got quickly closed and candles were lit. The gas fire was fired up, its juddering red flames adding a demonic veneer to the room. The sacrificial lambs, two pimply boys of about eighteen, goofy-grinned and rubber-kneed, were carried in and laid reverentially on a shag carpet. Ray the Rachel loaded the radiogram with Ricky Nelson records and splashed gardenia scent around the room. Cocaine then got razored up on a mirror, hashish sprinkled into sausage-sized joints, Mogadons downed with Johnnie Walker, dildoes oiled. Several of the old queens donned leather masks; enemas got filled with cheap frying oil...

The scene was set for the evil in man to run amok. The actors undressed, their naked bodies quickly glistening with sweat as the room heated up. The boys were stripped naked. Penises swelled like ripe fruit. My cue to exit. I went up the narrow staircase to my bunk bed and, with Ricky Nelson crooning in the background, read a few pages of a Dennis Wheatley novel before falling asleep.

The scream that woke me was so harrowing it could have been a castrato having his balls cut off. I scrambled out of bed. None of the lights worked. Another horrendous, tortured scream went through the house. I stumbled downstairs, scared at what I might find at the orgy. Through the window of the front door, I could see lights being switched on in the houses opposite, people standing in doorways.

I gingerly peered into the front room.

De Sade in his vilest imaginings couldn't have conjured a scene more disgusting. Candlelight revealed fifteen naked men, fat and flabby like huge beached walruses, lying in various states of stupor with their flesh, sweaty and oiled, smeared with cream, butter, strawberry jam – and blood. The two boys lay naked and inert on the rug. One was bound and gagged, the other covered in blood. He was groaning, obviously in great pain. A smell of burnt flesh pervaded the room.

I shook Ray. He was glassy-eyed, incapable of grasping any kind of reality. Then I heard the approach of a police car, siren wailing, and panicked.

No time to go upstairs and get my jacket, just get the hell out of here.

I ran into the back garden, climbed the fence and ran blindly down pitch-dark alleys. I heard a church bell chime 2am, and the screech of police cars arriving at the digs. There would be lots of ''allo, 'allo, 'allo, what have we got here then' when the police entered the front room.

I kept running until I came to a railway goods yard, bright beneath the jaundiced light of sodium lamps. Perhaps I could ride the rails back to the smoke, London? There were lots of railway wagons to choose from. I avoided coal and cattle trucks and found one filled with baled newspapers. I climbed aboard, slid the barred door shut, made myself comfortable and waited. I figured I'd either be in London or Scotland in the next day or so.

A jerky convulsion woke me. It was daylight and the wagon was on the move. Iron wheels squealed and screeched, a muscular power surging through the train as an engine up front huffed and puffed, eating coal and gaining speed.

I got lucky. The train went south. Eight hours later, I exited the wagon at Kings Cross. For weeks I worried that the Queens orgy would make the newspapers and I'd get implicated, but the story didn't even rate a line in the Screws of the World. A couple of years after, I was over Victoria Park way, and bumped into Ray. The kinky so-an'-so was sussing out the gent's lavatories, looking to chat up boys for a quick grope in the bushes. He was no longer the wavy-haired, coiffeured and manicured poofter of old. He was pale and haggard, just back on the streets from a two-stretch in Wakefield, for sodomy and GBH. As for the infamous night in Halifax, Ray recalled the incident.

"We were all slewed out of our brains," he said. "For a laugh, I took the shade off a table lamp and shoved it, bulb first, up the bum of one of the boys we pulled." A faint smile flickered across his pale lips. "I dunno, without finking I switched the light on."

His face flushed with colour. He grinned. "Alan, it was unbelievable. In the dark room, the kid's balls lit up bright red like a pair of Christmas tree ornaments."

I stood across the road from the Carlton among flowerbeds and trees that avenued the middle of the Croisette, intimidated by the hotel's palatial grandeur. I watched the endless convoy of Ferraris, Rollers and Bentleys purr to a halt, disgorging upper-class twats – puppets cocooned from reality by their wealth, all immaculately dressed like dummies just escaped from a Harrods window. I checked for police. Every five minutes, a gendarme would stroll by the front entrance and nod briefly to the harried doorman. The doorman could have been a general in the French Army, so impressive was his uniform of bottle green, piped with miles of what looked like gold marzipan. He was definitely the governor of the forecourt, whistling up cabs, snapping orders at bellboys to load or unload luggage, all the time casting his beady eye on everyone entering or leaving the hotel.

I might have trouble with him, I thought. He's probably been trained to smell out poverty. If he stopped me I'd be Valentine Xavier, American actor and friend of Jean Assouline, at the hotel to meet with... I couldn't think of anyone French who was famous, except General De Gaulle. Then I remembered Francois Truffaut. I'd just seen his *nouvelle vague* movie, *The Four Hundred Blows*, at the Everyman in Hampstead. A bird I chatted up at the Florida club in Leicester Square treated me. I thought the film boring and Hampstead a right toffee-nosed place.

Time to hit the hotel. I stepped into the road looking the wrong way, pre-conditioned, I suppose, to English traffic coming from the right. There was a tremendous screech of brakes, and I almost wet my pants with fright. A Lamborghini, top down, bright Italian red, the driver a kid the same age as me, had just slewed to a halt, nearly hitting me. My fault. How the hell could a bloke so young afford a car that cost more money than I'd make working down the docks until I retired? He started yelling at me, waving his arms while behind the Lamborghini, the traffic snarled. Horns blared.

Jesus, so much for quietly slipping into the Carlton.

I was tempted to grab the driver, pull him out of his fancy car and start throwing punches, but saw a gendarme threading through traffic towards the Lamborghini.

"Fuck you," I mouthed at the driver, despising his wealth.

I quickly jinked through stalled traffic to the pavement. The doorman and I were now a yard apart. Am I in or out? He pulled open the glass door and touched the peak of his hat in salute.

"*Bonjour, monsieur*, welcome to the Carlton hotel."

I passed into the foyer immediately, the street noises faded and I became embalmed in a very expensive hush. Looking at the magnificent, yet ludicrously overblown, Baroque bullshit of the hotel's interior reminded me of a comment my dad once made.

"There's no point in staying at a posh hotel," he said. "I mean, you can't eat the carpet or the wallpaper, can yer?"

The fact he never even took his family on holiday, let alone to any hotel, added futility to the observation.

The first thing that really caught my eye was the luggage waiting to be taken up to rooms or out to waiting cars. It was a veritable dead zoo of skinned animals: pigskin, elephant, crocodile, cow, alligator, zebra, horse, and every imaginable serpent from cobra to python. None could have imagined, while basking the banks of the Nile or slinking through jungle shadows, that they'd end their days stuffed with banknotes and petticoats.

I set off in search of a bar, wading across the deep carpet, marvelling at the glacial coruscations of the crystal chandeliers; the silk walls; the ceilings, ravished with rococo swirliques that convoluted from extravagant foliage to wide-eyed sea monsters. The Babylonian colonnades had as their capitals a flourish of palm leaves, and the hand-painted panels in the chinoiserie manner depicted Oriental ladies fondling monkeys.

I found a bar. The place was packed and smelled of Gauloises and money. No-one here worried about next week's rent. Fur salesmen, tycoons, and film producers with pouty birds, wheeler-dealers. In the pockets of shadow at each corner, rich old women hid their decay as they nursed their poodles. The barman performed like a dervish, windmilling bottles and conjuring glasses of champagne. Martinis and colourful cocktails were instantly snapped up by a continuous line of irritable waiters, to be arrayed on silver trays and then waltzed to tables congregated with customers squawking like parrots.

I stood at the bar for ten minutes, feeling more and more invisible as the barman ignored me. Perhaps I didn't have the veneer of wealth or looked a bad tipper. Finally, after I yelled and arm-waved signals at him, he confronted me, glowering with attitude. He didn't ask what I wanted to drink. He just stared at me.

"Is Jimmy or Albert here?"

He looked surprised. "Who wants to know?"

"I'm a friend of Jean Assouline."

This defrosted the attitude. "I'm Jimmy." His voice lost its plummy pretension and he sounded like a Londoner.

"Jean told me—"

"Look, kid," he interrupted. "This is rush hour." He waved his hand at the waiters lined up at the bar, who were impatiently waving bits of paper with drink orders. "Come back at four," he said. "I'll be off duty. Use the back entrance and come to the servants' quarters."

He turned away and began flourishing bottles like they were Indian clubs.

Chapter Nine

Three hours to kill. Out on the Croisette, the traffic was snarled, the pavements packed with rubberneckers. I'd look for a bookshop, get a bite to eat and maybe roll up my trouser legs, sit on the beach and have a paddle. My first setback came with the paddle. Turned out all the beaches were owned by the major hotels and charged a fortune for a deckchair on the sand, so I was reduced to simply staring at the gorgeous girls and speedboats from a distance.

I headed away from the Croisette and found a bookshop on Rue d'Antibes. Apparently Cannes had a fair-sized English population; there were racks of London newspapers. I bought the *Daily Mirror*, even though the price was outrageous. I could catch up on the football scores over lunch. I also bought a sketchbook, and a box of twelve Caran d'Ache coloured pencils.

Now to find a café and relax until four, I thought.

Apart from fish and chips, it would never occur to me to eat fish. Growing up, fish was eaten every Friday. It was something to do with Jesus and getting crucified, but I never did find out what. Cod was the only fish. My mum would boil the oily cod in milk and water, until it became a glutinous mush. Lurking inside the grey flesh were bones waiting to puncture, and get trapped in, the tender lining of the throat.

Being a finicky child, I'd pick around the fish, removing these bony spears.

"Stop messing about with yer dinner," my mum would yell. "You're picking the fish to death. Eat it all up and don't leave no bones, they're good for your brain."

Worse than bones was the rubbery black skin that tasted and looked like phlegm. My mum insisted it was the best part of the fish, rich in just about everything needed to keep away colds and flu.

"You're not leaving the table until your plate is clean," she told me.

There was no way I could eat the skin without throwing up, so I'd slip it into my pocket, then sling the slimy stuff away when I went out on the streets to play. Problem was, all my clothes stunk of fish and, as dry cleaning was unheard of, I began to lose friends.

My disregard for fish was about to change radically, though, at a restaurant called Poissonnerie de la Méditerranée, off Rue d'Alger. As I walked past the place, an aromatic smoke poured out from the open windows of the dining room. It was a smell of such seduction, it stopped me in my tracks. Customers at tables outside on the pavement were eating whole fish grilled to a beautiful blackness and served on a bed of lettuce, ornamented with wedges of lemon. Inside, I could see a pair of chefs working at a wood-burning grill, laying fish of various shapes and sizes onto the flames, dousing them in oil and lemon juice, then placing twigs on the embers underneath, which produced a rolling smoke that smelled of pine.

A chalkboard at the entrance showed Sardines – Hareng – Loup Grillé. I went inside and sat at a table away from the street, out of view of patrolling police. The table had a tablecloth. This bothered me; restaurants with tablecloths were probably way too expensive for my pocket. As I thought about getting up and leaving, a waiter – a lovely little white-haired man just like Edmund Gwen in *Miracle on 34th Street*, came to my table.

"*Bonjour, monsieur.*"

He handed me a menu, ornately decorated with anthropomorphic lobsters dressed up in evening suits and ball gowns. I guessed they were going to the opera.

"*Excusez-moi, quel est le poisson?*" Here my French ran out, and I pointed to the table where a man and a woman were eating whole grilled fish.

"Is monsieur English? The fish is *loup* – sea bass."

He shuffled off to the kitchen and returned holding an example, a beautiful, metallic-grey fish. He tilted it, allowing the light from the street to glitter along its scales. He held the fish to his nose and sniffed the whole length of its body, allowing little ums to flutter from his mouth, while his eyes rolled in their sockets. If he'd been sniffing Brigitte Bardot, I don't think he would have been more excited. He held the fish close to my face and pointed to its eyes – black, circled by a pale yellow. "See these noble eyes?" he said. "They still hold the colour of the morning sunrise."

A beautifully eloquent way of saying the fish was fresh. I ordered the sea bass.

"Wine of course, young sir?" offered the waiter.

I had been thinking of ordering a lager. "A Clos Sainte Magdeleine, or perhaps Coteaux d'Aix-en-Provence?" he suggested.

I didn't have a clue. Bass Ale or Ind Coope bitter, yeah – but wine... Well, it was another language. The waiter brought two bottles to the table, both chilled, then set two glasses on my table. With all this unaccustomed fuss, I began wondering if he didn't think I was someone famous, maybe Adam Faith. He poured a small measure of the Clos Sainte Magdeleine, swilled it around the glass and handed it to me.

I'd never tasted white wine, didn't know whether to sip or gulp it. Gulping was more masculine, I decided. The wine tasted like medicine. But then a miracle happened. After a few seconds, its complex poetry of smoke and fruit trafficked and galvanised my taste buds. The icy liquid hit my stomach and the gentle warmth of alcohol fired throughout my body. It was simply delicious.

I nodded approval. My glass got filled.

Sunlight danced within the pale liquid as the outer surface of the glass frosted and, after a few seconds, the condensation beaded and turned to tears that rolled slowly down the stem, pooling onto the table around the base.

I'd never seen a glass cry. Entranced, I pulled out my tracing pad and coloured pencils and sketched it as I waited for the arrival of the *loup*.

The waiter laid the fish platter reverently before me as though placing a holy relic on an altar. He emptied a small glass of Armagnac into a metal ladle, set fire to it, and poured the flaming liquid over the sea bass. He stepped back and bowed courteously, to await my approval.

"*Merci beaucoup, trés bon, merci,*" I said, gaining confidence in my French usage.

The waiter returned to the kitchen as I sat beguiled by the dance and flicker of the brandy's blue flames, but worried about just how much this poncing about, setting fire to fish and bowing and scraping, was going to cost me. I fingered my francs, just to reassure myself they were still in my pocket. Famished, I grabbed a knife and sliced the fish open from tail to tonsils, then lifted a chunk of pearlescent flesh and crisp, black, aromatic skin and mangled it into my mouth. Normally with food, the idea was to bolt it down as quickly as possible. Nine times out of ten it was tasteless, often revolting, with mealtimes simply a reason to fill up one's belly as quickly and efficiently as possible – a necessary inconvenience between playing snooker and looking for trouble. But the fish was a divine revelation – like seeing a Van Gogh for the first time; watching Stanley Matthews dribble; hearing Elvis's 'Heartbreak Hotel'. It was that good, each mouthful exploding with new subtleties of taste and surprise parcels of flavours; and with the wine, the whole meal became an unforgettable experience. Finally, with the fish reduced to a pair of accusative eyes and a skeleton, I continued with my drawing of the glass, filling in shadows, smudging on yellow crayon for sunshine, until it looked finished.

The waiter arrived to collect my plate.

"*Monsieur*, dessert, coffee?" he asked, then saw the drawing propped against the wineglass. "Ah, *monsieur* is an artiste. The drawing is *trés bon*, very good."

He collected my plate and hurried into the kitchen. I sat back in my chair, and I'm thinking, life don't get much better.

Here's me, a bleedin' docker getting called an artiste. I'm free as a bird, sitting in Cannes in a fancy restaurant, eating flaming fish and sipping Clos Saint Mag-something-or-other... Jesus, if the gang back home could clock me now, they'd shit a brick. Then, to spoil my reverie, I see the waiter and he's not just carrying *l'addition*, he's accompanied by a tall bloke, fattish and dignified with pomaded wavy black hair, dressed smart in a grey double-breasted suit. His face was dead-white, as though he had an aversion to sunlight, dotted with tiny black eyes like a pair of olives stuck in uncooked dough.

A cop. My pulse started banging as a cold sweat prickled the back of my neck. I checked the door for a quick exit but a waiter was stationed there, knocking on the head any chance of doing a runner. Anyway, I had my *papiers* story down pat. I'd lost my passport, I was in Cannes on vacation. The two arrived at my table and stood there about as solemn as a pair of church candlesticks.

The waiter bowed. "Monsieur L'Artiste, may I introduce to you Monsieur Reboux?"

We shook hands. He wasn't a cop. His hands were long and graceful, soft like putty: he'd never done a day's hard work in his life.

"*Monsieur L'Artiste*," the man said to me. "I am the owner of Poissonnerie de la Méditerranée, the most famous fish restaurant on the Côte d'Azur. May I view your illustration?"

For a second I was flummoxed, the word illustration being unfamiliar. Then I realised: he was talking about my drawing. So, I handed it to M. Reboux. There was an impressed silence for a few moments as they both studied the sketch.

"*Monsieur L'Artiste*, is the drawing for sale?" queried Reboux.

Why not? Sensing the possibility of a nice little earner, I figured it had to be worth twenty francs – three quid – but, before I could respond, Monsieur Reboux expanded his own proposition.

"Sell me the drawing and undertake a commission to illustrate a lobster for our new buffet menu, I'll pay you fifty francs and your meal will be complimentary."

"It's a deal," I barked, his sentence barely finished. "Bring on the lobster," I added, with a confident yell.

We embraced upon the closure of the transaction. I sat back at the table, my wineglass got filled and, with a surgeon's punctiliousness, I laid out my pencils and sketchpad. The lobster arrived, set on a beautiful Provençale fishplate. Fresh out of the water tank, it looked like it had taken to practising bondage, every limb and appendage secured with elastic bands. The only thing it could move was its curiously shovel-like mouthparts that fluttered in a constant state of anxiety.

I stared at the lobster, perusing its crusty shell, the beady eyes, spindly legs all askew, the heavy corrugated pincers. It looked more like an old, rusty, discarded carburettor than a living creature. In fact, it was hard to imagine inside its shell beat a tiny heart and, as it lay on the plate and stared out into its unfamiliar surroundings, it must have known death was close at hand.

Now to earn the fifty francs. I warily removed the elastic bands and immediately the lobster thrashed erratically, like an overwound clockwork toy. Its legs, claws and tail began clanking and banging noisily against the plate. If M. Reboux hadn't grabbed the creature's abdomen to apprehend it, the lobster would have scurried off the table, out of the restaurant and followed his antennae down to the Mediterranean. Tentatively, I began to scribble a rough outline of the lobster, watched by waiters, a gathering of diners, curious passers-by and M. Reboux, who enjoyed placing breadsticks between the lobster's snapping pincers and yelling "Olé!" each time a stick got neatly scissored in half. In-between his yells, he waved the lobster in front of the audience and, in staccato bursts of French and English, raconteured an anatomical and gastronomical lecture on the class of crustacea.

"*Mesdames et Messieurs*. May I introduce to you the queen – the empress – of the aquatic cornucopia of the Seven Seas... The exotica, erotica of submarine edibles... *Homard*, the lobster."

He held the armoured creature, with its active pincers, high above his head. Then, with great theatricality, he began sweeping it to his left and right, diving and climbing the poor thing like it was a toy aeroplane.

"*Homard*, of the class Crustacea. Latin for hard shell. Genus: *Homarus*... The noble lobster is not a fish, it is an *anirneux*, which breathes through gills in its thorax and, like the tax inspectors for our government, it has no backbone."

The joke got a hearty laugh from the ever-enlarging audience crowding at the open window. The only problem with M. Reboux's discourse was, I couldn't get a good view of the aerobatic lobster. I had to guess how the antennae fitted to the head and how many legs it had.

"The animal has poor eyesight," he went on. "Its eyes are compound, made up of hundreds of lenses, but sadly its vision is pathetically poor. He is the Mr Magoo of Marineland, moving in a world of one-dimensional shadows, a realm of chiaroscuro. But don't anguish, for this crustacean, it's no easy meat for prey by any means, with its gigantic antennae and sensory hairs covering its body. It has a built-in early warning system, able to detect chemicals and movements in the water informing it of dinner, or danger. Despite heavy armour, the lobster is no slow-coach, either with its eight thoracic legs for scooting along the sandy seabed, and a powerful fanned tail for propelling itself through the water."

M. Reboux had confirmed the number of legs and was fast doing for the lobster what P.T. Barnum did for Tom Thumb. He'd sold the place out, every table filled by attentive customers, with my little waiter serving everyone tiny dishes of sliced watermelon, green figs and black olives.

"*Mesdames et Messieurs*, why did God bestow the lobster with an armoured shell? To protect its most sumptuous asset: the tender meat of virginal whiteness, lodged within its segmented tail – meat of a buttery texture, of sublime sweetness and erotic, oceanic saltiness. Meat of a melting deliciousness, unique among the proliferation of God's creatures. All our lobsters are caught locally, and we only serve hen lobsters – for the female of the species, as with all species, is more tasty, more succulent..."

He paused to slather his wet tongue around his mouth and got a laugh.

"... if you know what I mean."

Reboux smiled lasciviously and winked. He turned the lobster, underside facing the audience, and pointed to feelers running beneath the abdomen.

"These are swimmerets. In a female, they are soft; on the male, hard. Also, the female has a smaller tail. And how should we cook our lady lobsters? Not by boiling them, that would

be sacrilegious. You end up with water tasting like lobster and lobster tasting of water. Here at Poissonnerie de la Méditerranée, our chefs slowly and lovingly steam the lobster on a bed of fennel, sealed in a cast iron marmite. I can assure you, not a *soupçon* of flavour escapes. Or, we brush the shell thoroughly with an oil de Provence and grill the lobster over the hot ash of embered apple wood – never flame. Flame dries the meat. Oh, what alchemy the heat bestows upon the lobster, magically changing its shell from a dull camouflage of black and green to a gorgeous royal red, a robe fit for a queen."

During Reboux's commentary I'd sketched the lobster, although I only got a good glimpse of the creature occasionally, as it was wheeled and dealed before the audience. I knew the anatomical correctness of the drawing was very iffy, so I went overboard with bright colours, hoping to distract Reboux from the fact that the antennae grew out of the thorax and the mouth, although aquatic, looked more codfish than lobster, the legs facing the wrong way, the eyes genus *homo sapiens*, not genus *homarus*. Maybe I could get away with it by calling it modern art.

Now came the moment of truth. M. Reboux came to my table.

"*C'est fini?*"

Without waiting for an answer, he grabbed the drawing and held it up, swivelling left to right to display it to the patrons. Adulation or humiliation? I'd know in a moment.

"The artist for this *art psychologique* is famous in England. At vast expense, Poissonnerie de la Méditerranée has brought him to Cannes to do a series of drawings for our new menu. *C'est magnifique? Non?*"

The diners joined M. Reboux in applauding. Many yelled, "*Encore!*"

M. Reboux hurried off to the kitchen, returned, and threw a live octopus on the table in front of me. Everyone laughed. This Reboux was not only a liar but a bit of a joker too.

Finally, I was forced to stand and take a bow. M. Reboux signalled for me to accompany him to his office. As I followed him, we passed a storeroom and I saw empty wooden boxes, marked Live Lobsters – Produce of Tunisia. Old Reboux was not only a liar and a joker but a con man as well. Now I wondered whether he'd try and screw me out of my fifty francs. In his office, Reboux pulled out five ten-franc notes from his wallet but, before handing the money to me, he insisted I sign the drawing.

"*Monsieur, comment vous appelez-vous?*"

"Alan."

"Alan, tomorrow come here at midday if you wish, and illustrate the octopus. We make good business. Yes?"

I signed the lobster, although it looked more like a Martian to me. The office clock showed 4:15pm. Shit, I'm late for Jimmy.

After giving M. Reboux a few ifs, buts and maybes, I bid him a hasty goodbye and left the restaurant, slightly dizzied by the wine. As I ran through the holiday crowds back to the Carlton, I couldn't help but be amazed. I'd just earned about eight nicker, and got a posh meal thrown in, and I'd been invited back the next day to illustrate an octopus. Must remember that word illustrate, I thought. So much more erudite.

Mind you, this wasn't the first time I'd made a few bob from drawing.

Way back when I was still at school, thirteen years old, I turned a few bob out of a naughty little fetish; made enough money to buy my own Italian bumfreezer suit and a pair of Winklepickers. After school, I loved hanging out at the local library, anything to save going home to Stalag Aldridge. I'd park myself in the reference section. The place was always good for a laugh, never short of a few geriatrics dribbling the free tea down their waistcoats, or the borderline loonies with their wrists and hands all twisted up, sloshing unintelligible words out of their wet mouths. Then there were the old war heroes, proud to have left chunks of their bodies on far-flung battlefields. The poor dumb bastards wore their medals proudly, but didn't have a pot to piss in.

Bert had been captured by the Japanese (or as he called them, little yellow bastards) in Burma, and was put to work on the infamous railroad. When he was too exhausted to keep pace, they cut the tendons behind his ankles. Unable to walk, he was left in the jungle to die. Poor old sod. He didn't remember how he got saved, but the experience reduced him to a gibbering idiot. King and Country now paid Bert a pittance: a war pension he collected from the post office, every Friday. You know, there were skuzzbags who waited outside post offices to mug blokes like old Bert.

Apart from observing the war heroes, loonies and dossers, I'd pull out books from the medical section. I enjoyed leafing through books on surgery and, in particular, reconstructive surgery. War wounds I loved, because they were particularly gruesome – bad photos of people with no faces, or burned beyond recognition, with pictures showing them after ten years of reconstructive surgery. They still looked like Quasimodo.

There was a section in the library with all the new weekly and monthly magazines. Each magazine had a wooden bar clamped to its spine, which was then chained to the library wall. If you thought of stealing a magazine, you'd need a bulldozer. I'd flick through *Picture Post*, *John Bull*, then *Flight and Aeroplane* – these latter two fuelling my daydream of becoming a pilot. Then I discovered *Vogue* or, more importantly, advertisements for ladies' undergarments: brassieres, corsets (of particular delight, all those straps and laces), suspender belts, girdles, and corsets with garters. Every ad sent me into a sweaty delirium. The models looked divine, not like ordinary girls you see on the street. These had nicely brushed hair, lips red and glossy and as big as pillows, eyes to adore. Each and every one of 'em wore this kinky, sexy, flesh-coloured armour, hiding breasts and other private areas that sent my hormones frantic.

I had to have the ads.

Tearing out each ad took about an hour, done with much loud coughing to cover the noise of paper ripping: Maidenform, Gossard, Silhouette, Bodyline, Trueform, Weldon, I got them all. When I arrived home, I went straight to the kitchen and grabbed greaseproof paper, then headed upstairs to my room, got a couple of 2B pencils and, in a state of excitement, locked myself in the lavatory, dropped my trousers round my ankles, and sat on the loo. I rested the *Book of Roses* on my knees, gently laid the Silhouette ad on top, and then placed the clear greaseproof paper over it, ready to draw my first nude. Starting at the head, I tremulously stroked lines, following the outline of her languid black hair. Next, the face. I pencilled in her eyes, haughty and taunting, the nose, and then the voluptuous red lips glistening with lipstick. The mouth was slightly parted, showing a hint of teeth and a tongue, moist and inviting.

Tracing was easy, yet I became totally immersed in the drawing. It was as if I'd stepped into the photo and was standing next to the model. I could feel the heat from her body; smell talcum powder, her sweat and perfume. She became my reality and reality a distant abstract. I drew the breasts naked, and as I'd only ever seen one pair, my mother's when she was feeding my younger brother. I copied those: huge, sagging with milk, the dark aureoles and nipples sticking out like a couple of Liquorice Allsorts.

"Alan," yelled my mum from the kitchen. "You get down 'ere, yer dinner's on the table getting cold."

Her shouting ruined my reverie. I was back in the lavatory.

Dinnertime, I thought. I bet it's mince. I hate mince.

"It's mince, your favourite. Now, get down here."

But I had to finish the drawing, obsessed to see it completed. So, ignoring my mum, I hurriedly traced in the thighs on each side of the body, down to the knees where the photo was cropped. Almost finished. But now I came to that part of the female anatomy, the topic of almost every conversation for all my pubescent mates. What exactly went on between a woman's legs? What did it look like? Myths and legends abounded. All of us, when much younger, had done the usual you-show-me-yours-I'll-show-you-mine scene with girls but I'd always felt cheated because there was nothing to see.

Only Billy Spicer reckoned he'd had a real gander at one. This gave the sallow, cunning, skinny little bastard a sense of superiority over us virgins – plus, he was the first in our gang to grow a moustache, all fourteen hairs of it, which added to his cachet as a bloke who had his way with the girls. Turned out he'd taken a peek at Mrs Briggs'. She was at least forty years old, and a widow. I guess not getting any pork sword for years finally sent her hormones berserk and she fancied Billy Spicer. How anyone could go for that pimply bastard was beyond me, but he reckoned she asked him into her council flat on the pretext of getting him to do some shopping for her as she'd sprained her ankle. So, in went Billy and before he could say Jack Robinson, she's sitting on the couch, skirt up, knickers down.

She says to Billy, "So what d'you think of it?"

Billy described it as a big whelk, all frothing and pulsating, surrounded by grey wire wool. Didn't sound too romantic. She ordered Billy to put his finger in.

"It won't bite," she said.

We gathered closer round Billy as he told us the story.

"It's got teeth," he said. "Sort of hidden inside the meat. But she promised not to bite me with them, so I stuck my finger in and wiggled it about. Inside felt all knobbly, like a table tennis bat. When I got my finger out, didn't 'arf stink."

He waved his finger under our noses and we all recoiled, catching a whiff of rotten fish. I made the decision there and then to forget girls and stick to football.

Now Billy lowered his voice. "I had trouble getting my finger out," he said. "It had tremendous suction, a vacuum what won't let go until a woman's satisfied. Mrs Briggs told me she'd got overexcited on a couple of occasions and actually sucked whole men into it, then blown them out as bubbles from her backside."

This was beyond belief. Whole men being sucked inside a woman? What a bizarre death. As I walked home that night, the idea plagued me. So how comes I hadn't seen any of these flesh bubbles floating about the streets? What about my Dad? If my Mum could turn anyone into a bunch of bubbles, it would've been him, always arguing with her.

Maybe she's losing her suction, I thought. After all, she's forty-five. But then again, things were always going missing at home: books, packets of cigarettes, my Hank Janson paperbacks... Maybe they were being sucked up by my mum's 'it'. Anyway, I was in no hurry to become a bubble. As for the drawing, I just scribbled a thick black Brillo pad between the legs. It was finished.

BANG! BANG! BANG!

The lavatory door almost jumped off its hinges.

"You fallen down the bog-hole? Get out and come and eat your dinner, or I'll put it back in the pantry and you can go hungry all night!" screamed Mum.

I preferred to go hungry but didn't need all the

aggravation, so I gathered up the tracing and book, pulled the lavatory chain, then stumbled into my bedroom. I hid everything under my bed and legged it downstairs to face the mince and the music.

Next day at school I showed the drawing to my mate, Jeff. First sight of it, he gaped. He got agitated and sweaty-palmed. He wanted to borrow it for the night. I told him it would cost him a ciggie, and I wanted the drawing back the next day, before assembly. I smoked the Woodbine on the way home from school. That night I drew three more nudes; only, this time, I shifted my studio from the lavatory to the shed at the back of the garden. Garden was an overstatement. It was really no more than seven-feet-square of threadbare dirt, tufted with a few stalks of grass and dandelions. The toolshed was a ramshackle conglomerate of bits of boxes, hardboard, found lumber and corrugated tin. It was perfect, because it had a small window overlooking the garden and rear of the house; I could see anyone who approached.

Over the next few weeks, I was a kid in a delirium of flesh; every spare moment was spent drawing nudes. I took them to school and bartered them for chocolate bars, ice cream, doughnuts, Swiss rolls and Tizer. Some kids even did my homework in exchange for a drawing. Often I'd get cash, two shillings a piece, and I'd sell as many as five a day. That was ten shillings: half a nicker. Business was booming. I gave up soccer practice, going to the snooker halls and the dance halls.

I drew 'til my fingers were numb, driven by the idea that it was easy money. Everything was going great. I'd just bought a suit and some shoes, and got at least forty drawings stockpiled, worth four quid at least.

I was on my way to becoming a successful businessman. At this rate, I could leave school before my fourteenth birthday. Then, one night I got home from school, and the front door was ajar.

Strange...

Normally it was locked and, as I wasn't allowed a key, I'd have to knock. Maybe Mum and Dad have been killed by a gas leak, I thought. Or burgled, murdered. Nervously, I pushed open the door. The house was unearthly quiet, no radio noise or Mum banging around in the kitchen, just a thick silence. I stepped into the hall and almost died of shock. The small hall led to a kitchen and family room; to the left, a narrow staircase went up to two tiny bedrooms and a bathroom. Standing inside the front door I could see every wall, the stairs, all the doors, even the ceiling were covered with my nude drawings.

The house was awash with tits and pubic hair.

My mind couldn't grasp what my eyes were seeing. I was speechless, panic-stricken. A thick ball of vomit surged into my mouth. In a dream, I walked into the kitchen – same story, nudes pinned up everywhere. I looked into the family room: naked ladies were propped against the radio, pinned to the fading wallpaper and sticky-taped to the curtains. Worse, my mum and dad sat in their respective armchairs in absolute stone silence, not even looking at me as I stood at the door.

Emotions of hate, shame and humiliation avalanched over me. I wanted to scream but only gargled, like a frightened rabbit. I turned and ran out into the night. For two days I lived rough in Liverpool Street Station, sleeping under benches.

In that time, I decided to leave home and school.

When I got to the service entrance of the hotel, the doorman bluntly informed me Jimmy had knocked off for the day. Turned out the clock at the restaurant was a half-hour slow, so I was over an hour late.

"Is Albert on duty?" I asked politely, sensing the doorman's Gallic intolerance of us English.

"Do I look like the hotel's employment officer?" he snapped back.

No – you look like a right berk, I thought, but I could see I'd get nowhere with this bloke, so I opted to go round to the front entrance. There was a different doorman on duty, same uniform, same miles of gold braid, but a surlier face parked on top of his shoulders.

He stopped me. "Is *monsieur* a guest at the hotel?" he asked, probably knowing I wasn't, blocking my way through the glass doors.

His stopping me took me by surprise, I'd expected to waltz straight in, still feeling a buzz from all the wine and adulation I'd got, back at the restaurant. Momentarily my mind blanked. Our eyes danced – his with suspicion, mine with panic.

Finally, "No, I'm meeting friends for drinks."

I stumbled the words together unconvincingly. Perhaps he'd stuck his hand out expecting me to bung him a few francs, but instead he continued the verbal tennis match.

"Which bar would that be, sir?" The sarcastic emphasis was noted.

We'd reached the critical point of our dialogue. I could either spit out an eff you and take a hike, or get bolshy and insist on entry.

"Albert's," I snapped, already taking a step into the hotel.

The doorman smiled, pulled the door open and ushered me through, bowing.

"Have a good evening, sir."

The bar was much as I'd left it – even the crowd, lots of the same faces, though the prevalent drink was champagne. The barmen were different. Hopefully one of them would be Albert. I got to the front of the bar and decided not to mess about trying to get served.

"Albert," I barked, my eyes darting between the three barmen to see which one responded. None of them did. It took a good five minutes before one of the barmen, freed up from serving the endless rotation of waiters, came over.

"You want Albert?" he asked flatly, with about as much charm as a rattlesnake. He had an unpleasant, sarcastic smile on his face.

It was one of those times I'd have loved to flash a wallet stuffed to the gills with hundred pound notes and tell the bastard I owned the hotel, and that he was fired for being a jerk. But that stuff only happens in the movies – although, legend has it, Frank Sinatra was in a Hollywood bar, Sorrento's, and the barman screwed up his bourbon highball. He got into a row with the manager, became so irate he bought the place and fired everyone.

"Yes."

"He's on duty in half an hour," he said, checking his wristwatch. "At seven." He waved his hand at the hordes of customers and grimaced. "He's in for a busy night," he added. "Your best bet, go to the staff changing room. He'll be there 'til 6:55 suiting up, having a smoke. Go out the hotel, round back to the service entrance."

He returned to the frenzy of waiters at the far end of the bar.

I decided to cut through the hotel. I figured it would be quicker and I could take a gander at the place. I pushed my way out of the bar into the foyer, where thick whirlpools of people swilled, giddy with gibberish; there were men in monkey suits, all curiously short in stature, and women dolled up like Christmas trees, glittering with jewellery and gaudy, sequined dresses that Liberace would have scratched their eyes out to own.

Picking my way across acres of floral carpet became a hallucinatory light show as the overblown décor, the gilt, the dazzle of cut glass, the flash of gold-embellished furniture, the explosions of flowers from bronzed *jardinières*, the walls with baroque flourishes of gold-leafed palms and cherubims, all scintillated and flashed with the reflections of candled sconces and chandeliers.

Towards the rear of the hotel, the crowds thinned. I took a wrong turn into a hallway of locked salons, found a door sign: *Défense d'entrer – Réservé au personnel.* I went through, into a corridor where the ambience changed instantly. The walls and carpet were grimy; the air, noticeably clammy, was thick with sour, soupy smells and I could hear the constant clatter of dishes. I hurried past maids slaving to load towels and sheets onto trolleys.

The corridor terminated with a service elevator. I'd have to go back – but then the elevator doors suddenly clanked open. The steel grille got thrown back, and a gang of room service staff came out, pushing trolleys littered with the debris of breakfasts and lunches. They barrelled straight at me, shouting and waving at me to get out of their way. I hastily retreated, lucky to escape through a swing door into a badly lit passageway.

I heard a crash and a yell. I'd hit a waiter, carrying a huge tray loaded with meals. No real damage – just a couple of dishes sent to the carpet, a few potatoes and mushrooms strewn on the floor – but he was angry as hell, and hurled all kinds of insults at me. He picked up the wayward potatoes and mushrooms, put them on the appropriate plates, lifted the tray and staggered off. He joined the endless convoy of waiters struggling in single file, sweating and swearing, taking meals at a run to the hotel's restaurants.

As each waiter passed, they cursed me. Some spat. I dodged my way through them and the heat, the noise, became hellish as I passed the hotel's huge kitchens. Waiters lined up at a service hatch, taking delivery of their orders. The activity was frantic, as food – meats running with blood, steaming vegetables, fishes, salads – got thrown onto plates by chefs, and fought over by the waiters. Food littered everywhere; the place was a pig's trough.

I found the staff changing room. A clock on the employees' time card machine said 6:55. I'd just made it. The changing room reeked of unwashed bodies and cigarette smoke. Along every wall stood tall, tin lockers, looking like coffins. No furniture, except a couple of benches. On one of them sat a man, half-dressed. He looked defeated and white-skinned, with huge, bloodshot eyes circled with black. He had a skin-and-bones body, but perfectly parted hair and a waxed moustache. He stared at me without saying a word.

"Albert? I'm a friend of Jean Assouline's."

I expected Jean's name to act like a magic potion and bring this bloke to life.

"Who says?" He stood and pulled on black trousers over his skinny white legs, wrapping braces over his shoulders.

"We did time together, La Santé. He told me you'd put me in touch with him."

He clipped on a bow tie and got into his barman's jacket.

"So what's your name?"

"Alan. Alan Aldridge."

Albert got agitated. "I don't know when I'll be able to get to a phone. I have to go. Where are you staying?"

"Nowhere right now."

"Find me at the bar at eleven tonight."

He hurried from the room, and I had four hours to kill. I saw no point in going through the doorman routine. I'd stay inside the hotel. Anyway, it had been a long day. I was beat.

I lay on the bench and closed my eyes.

I got woken up by a shout. The staff room was filled, waiters playing a noisy game of cards, some eating from bowls, all of them smoking. Nobody paid attention to me. I guess they thought I worked at the hotel. I got up. It felt like I'd been asleep for hours. I walked into the corridor, the clock on the punch-in machine said 12:40. I did a double-take. It still said 12:40. I'd been asleep for hours – five, in fact.

I hurried to the bar. It was packed. I saw Albert. Poor sod was working like a blue-arsed fly. I stood at the bar waiting for him to see me. When he did, he came straight over.

"l got Jean on the phone. He came here. Waited for you, ll until midnight. Wants you to meet him tomorrow afternoon, 2:30, here's the address." He handed me a piece of paper which I stuffed in my pocket. "You want a drink? Courtesy M. Assouline."

Albert smiled then. The miserable-looking bastard actually smiled. I saw why he didn't smile often. He had horse teeth.

"Champagne, Albert. Champagne."

He smiled a second time.

The bar closed at 2am, by which time most of the clientele were drunk. Even the women's beehive hairdos were falling apart. Albert spent a lot of time checking the cash in the register. Crafty old bastard was probably pocketing some. It was another forty minutes before we could leave. There was no point splashing out on a hotel. I'd made up my mind to sleep rough, either somewhere along the beach or back at the harbour. Shouldn't be too difficult to find an empty boat, I thought. Sleeping rough didn't bother me. I'd been all over England and slept in ditches, on railway stations, and one time in a funeral home. Albert offered me a bed and, although I fancied the boat idea, it occurred to me that I might be risking getting stopped by the cops. So I took him up on his offer, but then Albert never mentioned Millie...

We drove in Albert's '34 Citroen. The inside stunk of wine, vomit and more wine. I guess he must have got used to the smell. I screwed my face up with disgust when I got in. He asked me what the problem was. I told him.

"Your car stinks like a Turkish wrestler's jock strap."

He sniffed and said he couldn't smell anything.

We drove into the hills above Cannes. Looking down, the Mediterranean was dark and sinister. I pointed out hundreds of lights bobbing on the water, asking Albert about them. He told me they were fishing boats picking up lobster pots and catching octopus. I was glad I was in the car with him.

The house was tiny. It had one bedroom upstairs, a kitchen with a couch downstairs. I got the couch. Someone was snoring upstairs loudly. I guessed it was Albert's wife. He poured two generous glasses of brandy and gave me one. We drank in silence, broken only by the noise above us. Albert must have an ogre up there, I thought. I was nearly right.

"*Bonne nuit*,' he said, then climbed wearily up the narrow stairs. We'd emptied the brandy bottle but there hadn't been a lot in there. I was looking to knock myself out, though, because after my long sleep in the staff room at the hotel, I felt wired. I found an open wine bottle in the back of a cupboard, maybe four inches of liquid. I took a long mouthful. There were lumps in the stuff and I choked on something solid. I took a look in the bottle. It was filled with moths, all floating, some of them still alive. I wretched so hard, I expected my heart to come flying out of my mouth.

The snoring stopped.

I switched off the light and lay on the couch. It had been a long day and now moonlight stencilled eerie details in the room. Thanks to the brandy, I fell asleep quickly. I dreamed of lobsters and octopi, and me dancing with sexy mermaids. Someone was stroking my leg; I felt it through my dream. If it's a mermaid it's okay, I thought. If it's Albert, the little twat's in for a good kicking.

I opened my eyes. At first, I thought the Man in the Moon stood by the couch: a round, white face with piggy eyes, grinning like an idiot. Slowly, I realised it was an idiot – but man or woman, it was hard to tell. It stared at me, tongue between its tiny teeth, dribbling spittle. What the hell? It grinned even wider and touched my leg with a finger no bigger than a baby's. It wore a dirty bathrobe and, as it leaned forward to stroke my leg higher up, a huge breast fell out of the opening at the front. It was a she, and apparently horny. She exposed her second breast and then lunged for my crotch. I got my hands on her shoulders and tried to push her away. She was incredibly strong, built like a wrestler. And she smelled like one. The dressing gown fell to the floor as she straddled my stomach. I was no weakling but I was losing the battle. She had my arms pinned behind my head, as her breasts bounced around my face.

"Millie!"

Albert, the cavalry, had come to the rescue. He yelled at her for a full minute. She gathered up the dressing gown and waddled upstairs, all five feet of her. He apologised. Millie was his daughter. She should be in a mental institution, he told me, but she would be mistreated. I told him to forget it. I was tired, anxious to get back to the mermaids. He went back upstairs. I heard him talking to Millie. She was bawling like a baby. I felt bad.

Maybe I should have let her have a cheap thrill.

Albert dropped me at a bar off Rue Saint-Antoine at 2:25pm. The terrace was crowded, inside the same. But the place had character, lots of old-fashioned mirrors and carved mahogany, darkened and tarred by decades of cigarette smoke. I got a beer and wallflowered into a corner. I waited and watched the entrance, the bright sun silhouetting customers like a Balinese shadow play.

Jean came in around 2:45pm. He'd lost the grey veneer of prison and had a tan. His blond hair was even blonder. He looked like a film star: young Burt Lancaster meets Montgomery Clift. Too goddamn good-looking, everyone stared at him. He pushed his way to the bar and got a beer. Curiously, I found myself shrinking deeper into the shadows, unsure now why I'd travelled eight hundred miles to meet up with him. He was standing barely ten feet away and I couldn't walk over and embrace him. That kind of emotion was beyond me. I enjoyed my aloneness. I was a loner who'd always avoided friendship and its built-in responsibilities. I didn't feel comfortable embracing people and being embraced. I carried a sense of being different, an outsider, alienated. I could simply fade away and become invisible, merely a spectator – or, as Oscar Wilde put it, a viewer at the sanctuary of sorrow.

I realised, as I stood hesitant in the shadows, Jean wasn't the reason I'd come to Cannes. It was the challenge of the journey: a distancing from the humdrum routine of life in London, which had threatened to pasteurise me. Jean's good looks, his golden hair and impeccable clothes, his arrogance… They began to repel me. I didn't want or need his friendship. The only thing that attracted me to him was the irony of an impotent man being a gigolo.

I moved towards the rear exit. Let's sabotage having a good time and friendship, I thought. Who needs it? I'll catch the train to Paris tonight, spend a couple of days doing the Louvre and the Left Bank, then take my chances getting back to London by plane. But too late… Jean had seen me. Now I felt like an idiot, sneaking towards the exit. He pushed through the crowd, smiling his perfect smile, all bonhomie.

"Alan," he yelled.

I was struggling to throw off my indifference, my loner mantle, and show him some enthusiasm.

He grabbed me in a bear hug. "Alan, you came. I can't believe it."

I felt embarrassed. I didn't know what to say. He hugged me again, kissed me on both cheeks. A sense of panic overtook me. I didn't want to hang out in Cannes, stuck in a friendship with Jean.

I'll tell him I phoned London, my mother's ill. I'll have a drink, and then I'm going to catch the train to Paris and a plane to London. My mum doesn't have much longer to live. The excuse sounded pretty good in my head, and having it there put me in a good mood.

"Let's eat," gushed Jean, pulling me into a back room restaurant. The owner knew Jean, so we got the best table.

After lunch I'd tell him about my mum.

"This place is famous for its *fruits de mer*," he informed me, as he ordered.

Small plates of pretty food arrived at the table. Jean gave me a running commentary on each of the dishes, which included tapenade, black olives and capers doused in olive oil, freshly-caught tuna. Then came the plates of mussels, oysters, clams, scallops – all in their shells – with giant prawns and crawfish that looked impossibly red. We ate, we drank, we talked. I held in reserve my mum story, warming to the idea of staying in Cannes.

"So, Alan, how long are you going to stay in Côte d'Azur?"

"I'm not sure. I'm kind of illegal. No passport, no *papiers*. I'm persona non grata here in France. When I got out of La Santé, the cops put me on a train. They were kicking me out of France into Germany. I jumped trains, though, came to Cannes instead."

"I can get you a passport, but we'll have to get your eyes fixed."

"Eyes fixed," I echoed. "Like, what do you mean?"

"Like this." Jean put his fingers at the sides of his eyes and pulled, laughing. "I can get you a passport but the catch is, it's Vietnamese."

"Forget the passport," I said. "I'm better off without one."

He paid the bill and we drove around in his Bentley. He pointed stuff out – the best restaurants, the clubs with hookers, the bars to buy hashish and heroin. It all sounded flashy, but I found myself wondering if Tottenham were still in the FA Cup.

Any minute now, I'll slip him the sob story and be done with this gig.

"Where are you staying?"

"I've only been in Cannes one night. I stayed at Albert's."

He looked aghast, then began laughing. "Millie jump on you?"

"Not funny."

"Albert should have warned you, but he probably needed a night off."

"Night off? What do you mean?"

"She's insatiable. Got a screw loose and she's loose for a screw."

"Albert screws her?"

"She screws Albert."

"But she's his daughter."

"It gets them through the night."

"Jesus Christ."

We pulled up outside the Carlton.

"I've a film producer friend, works for MGM," Jean said. "He's in LA. I've got the use of his suite here. I'll be staying in Mougins for a few days, so I want you to use it. It won't cost either of us a sou. Okay?"

Jean handled everything at the front desk. I had no bags but the bellboy insisted on carrying my sketchbook and pencils. The elevator took us up to the fifth floor. The suite was palatial, with a sea view overlooking the beach. It had a bedroom, living room, bathroom, with lots of gilt furniture and Poussin landscapes on the walls. Jean ran through the hotel's facilities: spa, horse riding, tennis, swimming, massages, beach loungers – all taken care of. I was starting to think he was Professor Higgins and I was his Eliza Doolittle.

"Alan, relax, enjoy yourself. For the next four, five days maybe, I'm in Mougins, like I said, with a client. Here's my phone number there. Here are the keys to the suite. I'll see you whenever I can."

We embraced. He left and I sat in a Louis XIII knock-off, wondering what I was getting myself into. I had this strong, nagging feeling I was being set up but I decided to cruise my new digs. In the bedroom closets, I found an Aladdin's cave of clothes: silk suits, drawers full of shirts, socks and sweaters, everything neat and tidy. I went through every suit and found a wallet with two hundred-dollar bills and a couple of Diner's Club cards for someone called Saul Zaentz. I pocketed the money and pulled a chair over to the window. Wondering how many francs I could get for the dollars, I sat for a long time watching the endless parade of people cruising the Croisette.

The sun went down. I took a bath, and then spent an hour trying on suits before finally choosing a black silk lightweight, black loafers and a black T-shirt.

I went to the bar feeling like a millionaire.

Chapter Ten

"Jean says to take good care of you," said Jimmy the barman, who came right over to me as soon as I walked in. "What'll it be, sir?"

I got a brandy and ginger ale – and it was a real glass of brandy, halfway up the snifter, not like in English pubs. If you order a spirit there, they give you a thimbleful in a bloody great glass. I flashed the key at a waiter, told him I wanted to sit. Like a good little monkey he nodded, bowing, and escorted me to a table overlooking the Croisette. After an hour, it got boring just watching people swill drinks as they sat around joking and laughing. Anyway, I felt hungry. I thought about walking over to the Poissonnerie; I was in the mood to draw the octopus and get a little adulation. But I felt tired, not having had much sleep, thanks to Millie.

I decided instead to stroll into the hotel's main restaurant. At the front desk, I noticed guests were exchanging currency into francs. I got in line to unload the dollars I'd pocketed – but then I spotted that the cashier had to endorse passports with the transactions, so I sidled off to eat.

The restaurant was the biggest I'd ever seen, more like a cathedral. It reminded me of photos I'd seen, of the first-class dining rooms aboard the Queen Mary or Queen Elizabeth, lots of gilt, silk and angelic frescoes. I could hear the clank of expensive cutlery. Waiters were rushing round, setting fire to plates of food. A man in an impeccable monkey suit swung out from behind a potted palm to greet me.

"*Comment puis-je vous aider, monsieur?*"

"Dinner for me," I said.

"Ah, sir is American," he gushed.

"English."

"Of course. Is sir staying with us?"

I showed him my key with the room number on an accompanying brass tag.

"Certainly, sir. Right this way."

He manoeuvred between tables. I could've sworn he was on skates, he was so smooth. He sat me at a window table. Even before my backside hit the seat, an ugly-looking waiter with a poxed-up face appeared, wielding a water jug.

"*De l'eau, monsieur?*"

Before I could reply, he filled my glass. As he finished and departed, another waiter came to the table and took the white pyramid of cloth in front of me, deftly shaking it open and setting the napkin gently, with great ceremony, on my right knee. Two more waiters arrived, one handing me a leather-bound menu, the other a wine list. I knew exactly what I wanted, though. Steak and chips with a really cold lager. After an eternity, the menu waiter returned, his notebook and pencil at the ready.

"Steak," I said, when he asked for my order. "Steak and chips."

"*Stark, qu'est-ce que c'est?*"

"Steak. Meat. Steak, as in cow."

"*Stark azin car?*"

I pretended to milk udders, and then impersonated a cow. "Mooooooo."

He thought for a second. "Ah, *boeuf.* Beef!"

"Yes, beef. A beef steak."

He opened the menu and pointed to a section headed *VIANDES – BOEUF.* I looked at my options. *Rôti de contre-filet, Steak au poivre, Entrecôte à la Bretonne, Entrecôte à la Bordelaise… Entrecôte Grillée Châteaubriand…*

There were more choices but I was tempted to go for *Steak au poivre,* because steak was the only word I understood.

"*Poivre, qu'est-ce que c'est?*" I asked.

"*Poivre* is pepper."

Forget it, I thought. What I wanted was a steak cooked like I got at the Como Café. Tony the chef took a slice of meat, dropped it into hot fat and fried the shit out of it. It came up looking like a piece of burnt boot leather. Served with chips. The meat tasted like leather too, but bung the old sauce all over it and, for three shillings, you got yourself a right blowout.

As I wasn't paying, I thought I'd choose the most expensive of the choices on the menu, except there were no prices listed. Most places I'd eaten in, they started with the cheap dishes, like egg and chips, at the top. As you worked down the list, so the prices went up. Usually, the last entry was a mixed grill – steak sausage, lamb chop, a bit of liver, beans, tomatoes and chips.

"*Châteaubriand Sauce Béarnaise, s'il vous plaît,*" I said.

The waiter shook his head and rolled his eyes in despair, curling his lips like he had a sour taste in his mouth.

"*Châteaubriand est pour deux personnes,* sir," he said.

I pondered the menu, then forcefully poked the word châteaubriand.

"Châteaubriand and chips!" I exclaimed, loud enough to have the other guests staring at me.

The waiter looked flustered. "Cheeps?" he said, sounding like a bleedin' canary.

The maître d' showed up. "Is everything okay, monsieur?"

"I want chips with my *châteaubriand*."

"Cheeps, monsieur?" queried the maître d'.

"Let me have your pen," I asked him. He handed it to me. I drew a couple of circles dotted with eyes on the tablecloth.

"*Pommes de terre. Comprenez?*"

The waiter and maître d' both nodded. Now I drew a knife. I made out to pick up the knife. I might have lost them at this point. With the knife, I pretended to cut the potatoes into pieces. I then drew chips.

"*Pommes frites*," they both said at the same time. "*Pommes frites. Bravo, monsieur.*"

They both hurried off. A couple of ladies at the next table clapped and smiled at my performance. I bowed a thank you. The wine waiter came to the table next, all dapper in a green jacket adorned with silver-wired grape motifs. He was extraordinary, in that he had bushels of black hair sprouting from his ears and nose, really unattractive. He bowed obsequiously.

"Monsieur, my name is Robert. I am your sommelier this evening and would like to recommend some superb wines to accompany your Châteaubriand. Excellent choice. King of *le boeuf.*"

He spoke excellent English. This would be easy.

"I recommend the 1957 Château de Beaucastel Châteauneuf-du-Pape," he went on. "It is a most noble, full-bodied wine. Or, if you prefer something more fruity, then the 1952 Paulliac is excellent. Lastly, the Château Val Joanis from the Côte du Luberon is exquisite."

Before I could make a choice, the *viandes* waiter arrived back at the table, in a state of agitation. "*Pardonnez-moi, monsieur. The châteaubriand... Quelle...* Um, how like you to be cooked?"

Cooked? Nobody had ever asked me how anything should be cooked before. I didn't understand the question.

"The meat can be cooked rare, rare-medium, medium, medium well and well-done." At the mention of the last, he screwed his face up, as though it were an option of disgust.

"What is rare?" I asked.

As the waiter shuffled his English language deck to find the right words to answer me, the wine waiter came to his rescue. "The rare, the meat is seared on the outside, but bloody on the inside," he explained.

Didn't sound too appetising.

"Medium is more cooked," he went on. "Well-done is an insult to the chef."

"I'll take medium."

"*Merci beaucoup, monsieur,*" said the waiter, then hurried off to the kitchen.

"I'll take a glass of the first one, the Borstal," I said to the wine waiter.

"I am sorry, sir, we only serve that wine by the bottle."

"Okay, I'll take the bottle."

And off he trundled. Right on cue in this pantomime parade, the maître d' arrived. He held a plate under my nose. On it was a raw piece of meat leaking blood. Jesus, that's what being cooked medium looks like?

"Is it okay, monsieur?"

"I'd like it cooked more."

The maître d' looked puzzled. "More than medium, that I would not advise, sir. But how you like the meat?" He waved his hand over it for my approval. But I didn't catch on.

"I like it brown, not red."

"The brown, not the red?"

By this time we had both lost the plot. A looker from the next table, middle-aged but with a great body, hormonal lips and a face that had seen a few nips and tucks, was witnessing the farce. She leaned my way, showing plenty of cleavage.

"Do you approve of the meat?" she said.

I looked at her, flashed on her breasts, the pouted lips, and her long legs.

"No, you naughty boy," she said. "The meat on the plate."

We both laughed. Definite possibilities there, my son, I thought. Probably thinks you're a rich young actor – and she's with a girlfriend who's not bad, either. Swag the two of them up to the suite, get naked, squirt magnums of champagne all over the place, go for a moonlight swim, smoke some...

The maître d' coughed. I gave the meat a '*bon*' and off he went. Right on cue, the wine waiter returned, holding a dusty bottle of wine.

"Monsieur, the 1957 Château de Beaucastel Châteauneuf-du-Pape," he intoned, with a reverence usually reserved for the dead.

A waiter placed an empty cut-glass decanter and a candle, which he lit, on the table. Robert deftly removed the cork from the wine bottle and sniffed it, sifting the scent noisily through his hairy nose. Next, he sniffed inside the bottle.

"Excellent," he muttered to himself.

He poured an inch of wine into a glass, swirled it around, held it up to the light, sniffed it and then drank, holding the wine in his mouth. He rinsed it noisily between his teeth before finally swallowing it, with much smacking of the lips.

"*Parfait!*"

Great, I thought. Now, how about sharing the wine with me? But no, Robert hadn't finished whatever ritual he was performing. He took the bottle and, holding the neck over the lit candle, with great delicacy transferred the wine very, very slowly into the decanter.

"*Voilà, monsieur.* Let it breeze for a few minutes. *Merci beaucoup.*"

He bowed and left. Finally, I was able to have a drink. I reached for the decanter but a waiter appeared, out of nowhere like a rabbit out of a hat. He grabbed the decanter as if his life depended on it, and poured me a glass. I had no pretensions to understanding or appreciating the finer points of wine. After all, it wasn't an Englishman's drink. To me, it was quite simply how quick could I get it down my throat and get legless. So I took a couple of big gulps and my glass got empty. Like the chalice of the Holy Grail, it was filled right up again, thanks to my attentive waiter. It got emptied, it got filled. Emptied. Filled.

By the time the châteaubriand came, I was into my fourth glass. The maître d' arrived with a silver-domed platter. Behind him, a gaggle of waiters brought serving dishes of *pommes frites*; peas, still in their pods for Christ's sake; butter on a Sèvres dish; a boat of gravy; and another boat filled with Béarnaise sauce. The maître d' placed the platter on the table and theatrically swept off the domed lid. Blimey, the châteaubriand looked enormous – a big brown roly-poly piece of meat. Now the other waiters jockeyed around the table, anxious to place their dishes to the left and right of me, then retire. The fifth glass of wine definitely disconnected me from reality. Slowly the room began to rotate. The woman with the big breasts at the next table was also hitting the sauce pretty hard.

"So, how tender is your meat?" she hissed at me.

I turned. She was drunk, her dress up, thighs exposed. I could see a glimpse of panties. She smiled at me, opening those bronzed legs a fraction.

Blimey, I could see pubic hair. I began to sweat.

"'Ow you like your meat?"

It was the maître d'. I wanted to say, 'with hair round it,' but was too drunk to muster the words. He held a carving knife over the châteaubriand, moving the blade in increments of half an inch, one inch and one-and-a-half inches.

I smiled dumbly.

"He wants to know how thick you like your steak cut," gravelled the woman with the breasts.

Ah... I gave the nod to the one-inch. Uncut, the meat looked beautifully cooked but sliced, its insides were red raw. Blood oozed across my plate. Urgggh! Do they think I'm Count Dracula?

"In France men like zer meat bloody," slurred the busty bird at the next table. I didn't get the implication but later was told, Frenchmen pursue sex more vigorously during a woman's monthly period.

"Is everything okay, *monsieur*?" queried the maître d', cocking his head like an obedient spaniel.

It'd be great if you'd quit bothering me. I ignored him and got the first mouthful of meat into my mouth. I must be Count Dracula... Oh my God, I went to gastronomic heaven. This was meat beyond my imagining, flavours tumbling out of the tender flesh: salty and rustic, sweet and smoky. Ravishing to the taste buds, melting like butter in the mouth, it made me realise what an appalling catastrophe the steaks I'd had in England were.

The first slice went, aided and abetted by wine. So did the second, third as well, as I got into a furious rhythm of slurping gluttony, until meat and wine had been demolished. I felt giddy. The meat lay heavy in my stomach. Nausea shuddered through me. I'm going to throw up. I need fresh air. Can I make it to the Gents? I'm not sure. The room is on the move. Tables are circling me like dodgem cars. My stomach jumps into my throat; I'm close to parking a pancake. A waiter stands by the table, he's talking, smiling, but his voice sounds miles away. He's joined by the maître d'.

Now they're both mouthing off. I can't hear them; they look like goldfish gasping for air.

Air. I've got to get outside.

I stand. People's faces circle me like buzzards. The big-breasted lady looms into view. I get a close-up of her mascara, bloodshot eyes, gaping mouth slimed with lipstick. The tables tilt at curious angles; waiters blur, in and out of my view. I can hear voices echoing down a long tunnel. Somehow the ceiling, with its painted clouds and cherubs, is beneath my feet. Thick lumps of blackness fall over me. I keel awkwardly across the foyer and stagger into greater, absolute, darkness.

The phone was ringing, jangling louder than the matin bells of Notre Dame Cathedral. I woke up. My brain felt like it was nailed to a bed of razor blades. I had the vision of a codfish and my mouth tasted of rat fur. The phone kept ringing. I could hear water running in the bathroom; my clothes littered the carpet. The windows were wide open, two pigeons screwing on the balcony.

I fell back to sleep.

Next time I woke it was dark, the phone still ringing. The room had been tidied, windows closed. The bedside clock showed 10:20. Must be pm, I thought. I curled up and went back to sleep.

Now the sun slanted in thick bands into the room. The clock hands were at 7:00. Great, I needed breakfast. I went through Saul's wardrobe, picked out a black t-shirt, white pants and white loafers. I ignored the pile of messages by the door and went downstairs to eat. The maître d' of Châteaubriand fame didn't seem too pleased to see me, nor did any of the waiters standing behind him, menus in hand, ready to escort guests to their tables.

"Monsieur Aldridge, may I be of help to you?" he said, without a trace of enthusiasm. Maybe I'd puked up on his carpet. The memory of the previous evening had died along with about three million grey cells.

"Just me for breakfast."

He crinkled his face in puzzlement. "Breakfast, *monsieur*?"

I knew he knew what breakfast was. Dumb bastard was being difficult.

"Oui. Petit déjeuner. You know, *oeufs* – *pamplemousse* – *jambon*, and all that."

He smiled. "Monsieur, breakfast is served only until midday."

"Right," I said, raising my voice. "So, one for breakfast."

"Monsieur, it is seven-fifteen in the evening – *du soir.*"

Bugger me with a barge pole. I'd just lost twelve hours. I thought about strolling the Croisette, checking out the birds on the beach, but the idea I might get picked up by the police deterred me. I went instead to the safety of the hotel bar. Albert was on duty and looked delighted to see me.

"Jean's been looking for you. Here's his number in Mougins. Call him."

I rang Jean and he told me to wait at the bar, he'd join me in half an hour, he needed to talk urgently. Albert poured me a champagne on the house. I downed it, its frantic bubbles cleaning out the birdcage taste in my mouth. He refilled my glass. I gulped it down, and just as quickly my glass got topped up.

I'd better slow down, I thought, already feeling light-headed.

Two hours and four champagnes later, with no sign of Jean, I was having difficulty standing and holding onto the bar. I found myself wondering if alcoholism ran in my family. Albert hovered, alcohol distorting his face like a fairground mirror. He pushed another glass of champagne at me.

"Courtesy of the lady at the end of the bar," he said, slyly winking.

A right looker nodded my way, a dyed redhead, expensively powdered and painted, low-cut dress, diamond pendant dangling over her generous cleavage. Old enough to be my mother. I raised my glass to her, struggled to find my mouth and drank the champagne in one gulp, its bottled euphoria spidering through my system. I felt giddy, put my glass on the bar, misjudged the distance and broke off the stem. I urgently needed the Gents' room; on the way I'd stop, and thank the lady.

Now the bar, the crowd, the walls elasticated. The chandeliers liquefied and the floor heaved, like a storm-wracked ship. I keeled through the crowd, getting cursed as I knocked drinks over.

Someone reprimanded. "Don't eat pelican meat."

I was Alice, having stepped through a dark looking glass. I stumbled up to the lady in the low-cut dress. Her face had taken on the smudged look of a Bacon painting. I tried to thank her for the drink, but the muscular system of my throat malfunctioned and I could only garble something closer to Swahili than English.

I got grabbed forcibly by the arm, and pushed out of the hotel into the back of a car. It smelled of expensive leather. The woman from the bar sat next to me. She smelled expensive, too.

Who was driving?

Fragments of light flashed by the window. Darkness closed over me.

Someone nearby was yelling commands in German.

I squeezed an eye open. Reflections of candlelight squirmed, like fiery maggots, off every surface of an ornate bedroom. The woman from the bar lay naked on the carpet, white like a beached whale. She held her legs open like an invitation card. I saw an eye of red meat; centred thickets of dirty grey hair. A voice I didn't recognise, German accent, ordered me to piss on her.

I couldn't remember if I had a bladder. I was dead from the neck down.

Velvet fingers unzipped me, not hers, not mine. The voice insidiously demanded I piss all over the bitch. She arched her back, and the hairy eye leapt at me like some wide-mouthed fish, then fell back into the flowery bowers of the carpet.

I pissed, a wavering stream of urine that at first arched in every direction, over the bed, up the wall, the television; but, the unseen hand guided the torrent onto the sagging upholstery of the woman's breasts, her belly, splashing between her legs. She writhed, letting out a wounded animal scream, massaging the golden stream over her breasts and between her legs.

I passed out.

I woke wrapped in a goose duvet on top of an enormous four-poster bed in a stately bedroom. I could see chinoise jugs on carved commodes; a clavichord; turgid landscapes, three in all, probably eighteenth century. Sunlight splashed in oblongs of yellow on red silk walls. A clock ticked with antique authority. It signalled 6:10. Morning or evening?

I stumbled out of bed. I was still dressed. I looked out of the window. The villa stood high in the hills above Cannes. Between spidery branches of olive trees I could see the Mediterranean, flat as beaten gold. The radiant azure of swimming pools jewelled shimmering vistas of gardens, the enclaves of palatial houses. The air, hissing with flies, smelled of pine and mimosa. Far off church bells wrangled, as lizards scuttled among grapevines that crawled over every wall of the house.

I couldn't remember how I'd got to this place, my mind turned to toffee by alcohol. I had a severe hangover. Jean entered, without knocking, surprised to see me awake but not as surprised as I was to see him.

What the hell was going on?

"Alan, you're awake."

"I'm not sure."

"Jesus Christ. You don't look so hot."

"I don't feel so hot."

"Need some coffee?"

"I need some explanations."

The villa belonged to a wealthy countess (is there such a species as a poor countess?). Her name was Countess de Eze-Duville, or some such plummy bollocks. It was her *résidence secondaire* in Mougins, an ancient village perched in the hills six miles north of Cannes: an enclave for the very rich and famous. Jean was squiring the Countess for a few days, getting handsomely paid to support her arm at society events and procuring young boys to satisfy her voraciously kinky sexual desires.

We sat in the baronial kitchen sharing coffee. Jean claimed he'd pulled me out of the Carlton the previous night, and only just in time. The management had called the police. Apparently I'd urinated against the bar, a noble East End custom if a pub was too crowded to make it to the Gents. I'd not performed the ritual with any sense of surreptitiousness, however, but stumbled about, waving my pecker all over the place and spraying the patrons, sending everyone panicking behind the potted palms. I guessed I'd fucked up my chances of returning to the Carlton. The way Jean told the story, he made a point of emphasising I owed him one. If he hadn't shown up and hauled me to his car, I'd be in prison again, looking at a six-month stretch.

"Alan, I need a favour."

Blimey, this bloke don't miss a trick: one second sticking it to me about how much I owe him, then bang, wants a favour.

"Yeah?"

"Tonight I'm going to rob the house of one of the world's richest men. I need your help."

I lay in the absolute darkness of the Bentley's trunk, still hungover, bouncing painfully as the car drove to Notre-Dame-de-Vie. Up front, Jean was at the wheel with the Countess next to him in the passenger seat. She was unaware I was in the back. We were heading to the country estate of a man said to have legendary wealth. Jean described him as a magician, sorcerer and shaman of money; a man able to conjure creatures – basilisks, minotaurs, Beelzebubic goats, serpents – out of the darkness of his soul. By an alchemical process, he transmuted these factotums of his imagination into legendary amounts of money. Bewitching to women, he would barter – for food, houses and cars – his phantoms of cerulean blue; beasts of ox blood; stallions made of basketworks in ivory black.

A modern-day Midas, beyond wealth.

"You know, Alan, the rich feed off the blood, sweat and tears of the poor," Jean had said to me earlier. "All we're doing, in relieving this vampire of a couple of his most treasured possessions – a pair of black diamonds, each over fifty carats – is redistributing his wealth. He told the Countess he lays them on his eyes in bed and, when he sleeps, they bring him visions. Insights into even greater wealth."

Jean made the gig sound very mystical and noble, like Robin Hood, all this balls about taking from the rich to give to the poor. Talk about ironic, though: he was sitting there with his fancy Patek watch, a silk shirt, house in Monte Carlo, the Bentley and a fully-loaded Swiss bank account.

"The Countess will call on the gentleman this evening to pay her respects," he went on. "The man is entertaining a few friends from Paris. They will dine al fresco, on the patio at the rear of the house. There are no servants. The man lives as a recluse, protected by elaborate security systems. The Countess and I will spend half an hour chit-chatting, then make our excuses to leave on the pretence of attending a charity function at the Hotel de Paris in Monte Carlo. Half an hour will be plenty of time for you to enter the house. Take the staircase to the first floor landing. Go right, second door. With luck, you'll find the diamonds on the pillow. Take them and get back to the Bentley as quickly as possible. I'll take the stones to my fence in Monte Carlo. Alan, for the tickle I'll give you two hundred quid, as you Cockneys would say. Then, tomorrow morning, I'll drive you to Nice Airport and get you a ticket to fly back to London. It'll be best for both of us if you're out of the country."

Two hundred smackers. That was nine months of slogging my guts out down the docks. It also meant freedom, a chance maybe to get into the art game for a living. And going back to London? Blimey, I thought. I could be watching Spurs at White Hart Lane on Saturday.

The car smoozed to a halt. I heard Jean announce the Countess into an intercom, followed by the clanking of an automatic gate opening. The car cruised slowly uphill, crunching gravel for over a minute, then stopped. Doors slammed. There were greetings in French and Spanish, then silence.

I'd been in the trunk a total of fifteen minutes since Mougins, my claustrophobia rapidly threatening to overwhelm me. I had to get out, but could hear people laughing nearby. I clenched my teeth and waited. Finally all I could hear were the crickets. I pushed the clasp of the lock on the trunk. The door should've opened. It didn't. I tried again. It didn't budge. A nausea of suffocation pressed down on me. I frantically shoved at the clasp.

Again, nothing.

My system now went into a blind panic. I was being buried alive, asphyxiated, torn apart by dwarves. I couldn't care less about Jean and his diamonds. By a stroke of luck I found a tyre lever, shoved it hard against the clasp and the trunk door sprang open at last. Cool, pine-scented air flooded in, the demons vanished and the moon beamed down, big and benevolent.

Soaked in cold sweat, I climbed from the Bentley and stood on a stony, overgrown driveway. The house was nothing like I'd imagined. I'd expected one of the world's richest men to be living in something like Versailles, a vast pile of architectural confectionery with marble, formal gardens, peacocks strutting on manicured lawns. This place was small, gloomy, built of rough stone; it was covered with ivy, a rundown farmhouse. Maybe it was just the gatehouse, only the entrance was just as Jean had described: arched, with steel shutters pulled across double-glass doors, a statue of an old man holding a goat on one side. The house stood in darkness, guarded by towering cypresses like giant bayonets. Olive trees massed in the front garden and, dotted in among their trunks, stood sculptures – outlines etched eerily by moonlight.

I hesitated at the entrance. Committing burglary was a big step up from stealing cigarettes and dirty magazines from Matthew's, a local newsagent, but the money and the ticket home to London outweighed whatever conscience I had. Anyoldhow, in the East End, stealing from the rich wasn't so much a crime as a way of life.

The steel shutters creaked as I eased them wide enough apart to get through. I nudged the handle of the heavy glass door and it sprang open. Adrenaline raced through me as I stepped through into the uninviting gloom of a large storage area, a mausoleum of the bizarre.

Entering this stillness, I felt like an intruder into a kingdom of the uncanny. Everywhere, statues stared back at me, as though resenting my intrusion. Scary statues, they were: a

menagerie of hunchback cretins, huge alabaster heads bloated with encephalitis, or knobbled with leprosy. There were owls with two heads, a Venusian-looking character with saucer eyes and a periscope sticking out of its head while pushing what looked like one of those wheeled contraptions that paint white lines on football pitches. Only one statue looked like a statue. It was a muscular bloke, about seven feet tall in plaster, doing an impression of Elvis, T-shirt up round his chest and otherwise bollock naked. Sadly, he'd lost his cock. It was the kind of statue gay men stuck in their bathrooms. I'd seen a replica at Ray the Gay's house, and in an Italian restaurant. It was by Michelangelo. Or was it Leonardo da Vinci? Some famous Italian or another.

Apart from the looney tunes army of statues, the house stank but not unpleasantly. It was an aromatic broth of turpentine, paint and a sixty-French-cigarettes-a-day habit; of cooking, and cabbage. It was like a peasant's house. These were working-class smells. There was another smell that had me retreating to the car, though.

Dogs.

My fear of dogs far outweighed my fear of dwarves with sharp teeth. I'd been walking home from junior school, eight years old, short-cutting it down back alleys, when I was confronted by a snarling black mongrel, a curious and probably genetically unstable mix of Labrador and Pekinese. The huge mutt crouched, readying to spring, snarling and foaming. I swung my boot, hoping to kick the ugly bastard in the teeth. I missed – and the brute, which must have had a touch of canary in its genes, flew into the air over my flailing kicks and sunk his fangs into my face.

Worst of all, its upper front canines got snagged under the bone of my eye socket. Now the whole weight of the rabid animal was hanging from my head, desperately trying to shake itself free, getting angrier each time it failed. I grabbed its muscular body and tried to lift it, but I couldn't. It was too heavy. I grabbed its balls, which were bouncing against my chest, and squeezed with all my strength. The dog let out a throat-curdling howl. Our eyes met, being just a few inches apart, and the animal gave me a hurt look, as if to say, "Grabbing one's scrotum, ol' chap, ain't quite cricket." But it did quieten him down. I yelled for help, but being the East End, everyone ignored my plea, preferring to hide behind lace curtains and not get involved.

I had to carry the slathering hound home, over a mile. When I walked into my house, covered with blood and rabid foam, my mum took one look at me and said, "Alan, why 'ave you got that dog 'anging on your head?"

It was hard to come up with an answer. However, she quickly realised the gravity of the situation and certainly didn't lack ingenuity in her attempts to part fangs from flesh. Mum began by poking the dog in the mouth with a fork. In response, the dog shook its head violently, which was very painful for me. She then tried hitting the dog on the head with a rolling pin, hoping to knock it unconscious. It was a good idea, but she lacked the moral turpitude necessary to deliver a coup de grace, and simply bonked the dog's skull lightly, making it slobber with anger. She stuck darning pins into its ribs and let off mousetraps on its tail. Nothing worked. Next came her best idea yet: cayenne pepper on its balls and arse. Sure, it burned like hell – but the dog, anxious to lick off the offending powder, pulled my head into its crotch.

Not a pleasant experience.

By now, my face was totally numb. It had swollen to the point where I could barely see. Next came the enema, the family cure-all and my mother's favourite mode of torture when treating illnesses. A cold got a hot water enema; the flu, a black pepper and hot water enema. For constipation, it was a glycerine or syrup of figs enema. Skin complaints got black coffee; nits and fleas, mentholated spirits and hot water. For everything else, it was oil of paraffin. For the dog, Mum mixed a powerful concoction of horse liniment, eucalyptus and Coleman's mustard. It was a potion guaranteed to strip the nickel-plating off cutlery. She stuck the hose up the dog's backside and administered a bulbful of the mixture, straight into its bowels.

Whatever my mother had hoped to achieve, she could never have guessed the outcome of the enema. It sent the dog into a sexual frenzy and it started dry-humping my armpit. My mother, a good Christian, was horrified. She ran to the local phone box to call the doctor.

Doctor Boyce, seventy and shortsighted, arrived. The dog was fast asleep, worn out, a smile on its face, having had numerous ejaculations. The doctor grabbed the beast around the waist and tried to chloroform it. The dog retaliated, loosening a terrible explosion of mustard-exacerbated diarrhoea over the doctor, and my mum's best couch. The dog had sealed its own fate. The doctor, livid with rage, filled a syringe with morphine and administered it into the dog's backside. After a few whimpers, it died. The doctor gave my cheek a shot of painkiller and, at last, the dead dog got extricated. My face looked like the Elephant Man's: hideously swollen, the skin black and blue.

I've been wary of dogs ever since.

I moved cautiously into the gloomy entrance hall, the dogs a worry – but something else was seriously wrong. The place looked like a doss-house: newspapers strewn everywhere, pots, bouquets of paint brushes stuck in used coffee cans, canvases stacked against walls, posters of bullfights pinned to the walls. Steel shutters crosshatched every window. Who the hell would want to steal this junk?

There was a large room to the left of the entrance hall. The strong moonlight illuminated more canvases stacked against the wall, the ones facing forward mauled with childish scrawls. Every chair had miniature cities of books, boxes and papers piled on them. Across the floor, islands of rubbish littered the cheap raffia carpet. The rich bloke who lived here seemed to be buying up, big time, the work of a bunch of no-talent artists. I saw no evidence of wealth, no bureaux de Louis Quinze, no Sèvres bowls, no gilt stools by Pelagio Palagi... There appeared to be nothing of worth. A pile of rubbish.

Savoury smells of grilled fish wafted through the house. I heard glasses chink and laughter. At least Jean and the Countess were having a good time.

The stairs were pitch dark, a hostile darkness that seemed to thicken, as though the house itself battled my intrusion. Whether it was all Jean's gobbledygook about magicians, occult powers and astral-voyaging having an effect on me – or the bizarre bunch of statues at the entrance, my hangover, a touch of claustrophobia, or what – I felt extremely edgy. I was teetering on the brink of panic as the darkness and silence pressed over me.

I reached the stairwell. It gaped open like a huge throat filled with total dark, anxious to swallow me. I took a step up into the gloom, but a scraping noise close by stopped me dead in my tracks, razoring my nerves. I spun round. Across the hall, silhouetted by moonlight, framed against one of the large arched windows stood a man, watching me. Fear gnawed and set my heart banging against my ribcage. I froze, not daring to move, watching the watcher for what seemed like a month of Sundays, waiting for him to speak, to move, to betray himself. But nothing disturbed the leaden silence of the house.

Until I chuckled.

My eyes having adjusted to the dark, I could see the man was no man at all, but an unfortunate alignment of a wrapped package and an African sculpture of a head. I could make out details of its shell necklace, wide eyes and the serene expression on its face. In that brief moment I lost my bottle to go on, thinking I should quietly steal my way out of the house, walk the six miles to Cannes, get the bus to Nice Airport and take my chances on getting a plane back to dear old London. But again, the lure of easy money beckoned: it was my key to getting out of the docks, the East End, and renting my own gaff, trying my hand at becoming the next Uncle Sidney.

Hesitantly, I started up the stairs, each uncarpeted step creaking like I was in some ghost-house film. I got halfway, when I heard the shuffling approach of footsteps. I pressed myself against the wall, images of being caught flashing through my mind; of prison, the queens, slopping out. Candlelight flooded into the entrance hall below, peeling shadows from the stairwell and sending phantoms of orange and yellow scurrying and juddering onto the walls. A man padded across the hall below me, clutching wine bottles and holding a candle. If he looked up I was done for, nicked. But he didn't. He disappeared down a corridor that led to the rear of the house. Shadows quickly coagulated.

With a sense of panicked urgency, I climbed the rest of the stairs in utter darkness. On the landing I had to grope along a wall, feeling for the bedroom door, for here the shadows were clotted even thicker than downstairs. There were no windows, there was no moonlight. No detail.

Suddenly the house exploded with laughter. I could hear yells in Spanish and French. Then, candlelight gentled the gloom of the stairwell. Against its yellow blush, a shadow stretched, eerie and huge, over the wall alongside the stairs. Someone was coming up to the landing. A man, woman, witch, wizard, magician, sorcerer, demon, Nosferatu? I fumbled along the wall, found a door ajar. It had to be the bedroom. I stepped inside. It wasn't. It was just a white-tiled bathroom, pallored by moonlight. I pressed my ear to the door, listening. The house had gone pin-drop quiet, with just the occasional rheumatic creak from its ancient foundations. The partygoers must have gone back outside.

Time was running out.

I edged back out onto the landing, groping blindly along the wall until I reached the next door, surprised to see a faint light slivered at its base. My scalp crawled as I cautiously pushed the doors open and tiptoed into the bedroom. Books, prints, paintings and unopened packages lay across the floor and crowded the walls. A small lamp on a table glowed weakly. An enormous dough-coloured duvet covered by a vicuna fur quilt engulfed the bed.

On the pillows lay the two black diamonds, side by side.

A sudden violent and frenzied noise made me jump with fright. It was a large moth, battering at the window. I was shaking with tension. Perspiration began to pump out of every pore. I felt as much like a thief as the Archbishop of Canterbury. I gumshoed to the bed. I was surprised to find, lying on top of the huge puffy duvet, an envelope with my name scrawled across the front. I grabbed it and glanced inside. Talk about serious spondoolick. A thick wad of freshly minted French francs. Hundreds, mostly.

But why would Jean leave my cash in the bedroom? Didn't make sense, not unless he'd already split for Monte Carlo. One thing was certain, I wanted to wrap up this French gig, tout suite, and get me and my money back to London. So I gingerly lifted the diamonds off the pillow, wary of their supernatural powers. They were heavy and black as coal. The jewels seemed to suck in the meagre light from the bedside lamp, transforming it into brilliant flashes and splinters of fire that cavorted along their faceted surfaces.

Now to get the hell out of this morbid place.

As I turned to leave, one of the pillows flew off the bed, as though imbued with life by some sorcerer's spell. It leapt at me like a wild animal, hitting me in the chest. More shocked than scared, I jumped back, tripping over junk. I fell to the floor, dropping the jewels but still clutching the envelope of money.

Attacked by a pillow. What next? My imagination ran wild. I wondered if every object in the house was going to animate with life – clocks, tables, chairs, paintings, the weird statues – like some crazy Walt Disney cartoon, all of them trying to prevent me leaving with the diamonds.

As I started to get to my feet, the duvet and vicuna quilt rose up from the bed, briefly looming over me like a shaggy massif, then fell, engulfing me under their bulk. Suffocating, I frantically brawled my way out from under it and screamed. Or rather, I tried to scream. I only managed a pathetic gargle, because I'd seen on the bed, eerily etched by the wan light of the lamp, a half-naked demon with a baboonish, hair-shagged body. Its face was straight out of a Hammer horror movie: slit eyes, a pointed nose and a wide fang-filled mouth that swept upwards in a terrifying leer.

I gasped, muttered prayers seeking forgiveness and asking for the protection of Jesus Christ. I begged. Oh, Lord, there is no sin that cannot be forgiven. Our Saviour who died for our sins. Oh Lord, protect me in my time of need. My heart convulsed violently. I turned ice cold, sieving sweat. My intestines knotted as my bladder emptied involuntarily, with pathetic squirts.

The demon stared at me. I goose-fleshed, tried to stand and run, but my legs were leaden, emptied of blood and circulation. They were about as useless as a pair of farts in a thunderstorm.

Pandemonium!

The main light of the bedroom suddenly blazed on and Jean entered, followed by a swarm of people. He yelled and screamed rapidly in French, pointing directly at me as I shook with fright. He took the envelope out of my hand and emptied the banknotes onto the bed. It looked like the double-crossing bastard was turning me in. Now everyone got in on the shouting act, behaving like they were on a TV game show. Jean was acting as master of ceremonies, cajoling and encouraging the heated badinage, shaking his head furiously when guests spat words as he counted off time, "*une minute, deux minutes. . .*"

I hadn't a clue what was going on. It was bedlam.

Then a man yelled. "*Le Salaire de la peur!*"

Jean screamed with delight, jumping up and down as though he'd just scored the winning goal in the FA Cup Final. He threw his arms around another guest, a man, and gave him a congratulatory hug. Then everyone went into a paroxysm of hugging and shaking hands.

The demon stood. It was laughing too, hugging Jean as they exchanged words in Spanish. The entity then pulled off its mask and turned to face me. The man smiled and offered his thick, peasant hand to pull me up from the floor.

My jaw dropped. Only one man in the world had eyes that burned as bright and full of curiosity as the eyes that burned through me now.

PICASSO!

Chapter Eleven

Here was the world's greatest living artist, one of the most influential icons of the twentieth century, painter of the revolutionary *Les Demoiselles d'Avignon* and monumental *Guernica*. Picasso was surprisingly small, five-and-a-half feet in height, at most. He had astonishing skin, deep brown like Spanish earth, with not a wrinkle. He could pass for fifty-odd. In fact, he was eighty-two years old. But he had the eyes of a giant – huge, sloe-black, big as saucers and sequined with an inquisitive, yet vaguely diabolical, glint.

With the light on, I could see the full extent of the junk strewn around the vast bed: newspapers, books, magazines, fan mail (unopened), trampled prints, photographs, pots of paint... Clothes were strewn on the floor and piled on a broken-down chair that leaked stuffing. A large chamber pot served as an ashtray and target practice for Picasso's cigarette butts. He must have smoked in bed, then tossed the butts into the chamber pot. Except, he missed more often than he scored. There were fag ends littered all around the pot.

Picasso found a colourfully patterned shirt on the floor, pulled it over his strong, broad body, and encouraged everyone to follow him downstairs to the garden for dinner.

Going back through the brightly lit house, I got a whole new view of its chaotic eccentricity. The walls of every room and corridor were stacked two, three, four feet wide with canvases, some showing phantasmagorical creatures such as minotaurs, fawns, satyrs and hippogriffs. They were painted in a frenzy of brushstrokes, while nudes and female heads were executed with a gentler care. Apart from canvases, there were easels, rolls of paper, charcoal and chalk drawings, aquatints, linocuts, ceramics daubed with fish and owls, copper engraving plates, maquettes and collages. It was an Aladdin's cave of one man's madness, passion, and love.

In the hallway, I bumped into the dog of the house, a Dachshund, or sausage dog as they're called in England. He was taking a piss, leg cocked up against a painting of Jacqueline and what looked like a cubist rendition of an Afghan hound. When the dog saw me it lay rigid on its belly, nose quivering, baring its puny teeth, eyes bugged with apprehension. It looked like it was readying to attack, so I growled louder and swung my boot at it, wanting to stove its head in. The dog lurched backwards, avoiding the kick. It skedaddled on its stumpy little legs, tripping over in its haste to find its master in the garden.

At the rear of the house a table had been set up beneath the vaulted tangle of olive trees. Candles bombarded by moths flickered among bottles of wine, Evian water, and brightly coloured platters heaped with chopped tomatoes, sliced raw vegetables and simple, green salad. Picasso, at the head of the table, and the five guests, sat on a motley collection of chairs brought out from the living room. It was a picture of homely informality.

It wasn't cold and yet I shivered, my peed pants and sweat-soaked shirt clinging to me like drowned skin. I hesitated at the French windows, unsure if I was invited to the party, having just tried to rob King Pablo the Midas of his magic jewels.

Picasso stood and beckoned me to the table. He looked ordinary, like a local pharmacist, a gardener or a bank clerk, not an artist, until his huge black eyes swelled and held you in an hypnotic vice. Then you knew yourself a witness to some of the most extraordinary creative voyages of the century. Picasso shook my hand firmly, then hugged me, grimacing as he felt my cold sweat-soaked shirt.

"Ah, the boy with the cat face," he said, echoed in English by Jean as though he were a puppet operated by Picasso. "You could be a dancer with Ballet Russe. Diaghilev would've hired you even if you couldn't dance."

Everyone laughed but I didn't get the joke.

Jean introduced me to Picasso. "Maestro, Alan is a roast beef, a Cock-e-ney from London."

Picasso nodded. "London," he said. "I went once. A city of grey. They eat whale meat there. I met an artist, Topolkski, his paintings..." He pulled a face like he was sucking lemons. "Constable meets Jackson Pollock."

Everyone laughed except me. Again, I didn't get the joke.

Jean introduced the other guests. First, Henri 'Oojamaflip' (I didn't catch his surname). He was a saturnine and haggard, private-looking man described as one of France's leading auteur filmmakers. He perpetually chugged on a pipe as big as a flowerpot, the bowl a fiery cauldron of embers that spat sparks and belched out smoke in thick, rolling clouds that often hid his face.

"*Enchanté*, Alan," said his disembodied voice. "Your acting..."
Acting?

Before I could give this revelation any thought, Jean hurriedly interrupted Henri to introduce the next guest: Madame Maria Lissitsky or Livitski. She was a buxom woman in her sixties, wearing a flamboyant straw hat, smudged lipstick and enough jewellery to go on show at the Tower of London. She looked Italian, but was Polish aristocracy. She owned a publishing house and was a long-time friend of the late Gertrude Stein. I recognised the Countess. She flashed me the same toothsome smile she'd flung my way across the bar at the Carlton, along with buckets of champagne, until I got legless. Fragments of that night at her villa in Mougins flashed through my mind. I wondered if Jean had set me up to be her sex-toy-boy.

Next was Maurice. He worked as a designer for the House of Hermès in Paris. He looked weedy, thin-faced, scrawny-necked, ears two sizes too large for his head. He had no chin and his hair was brilliantined, combed back impeccably. Maurice was a marsupial-looking queer, with ratty teeth, squeaky voice, and shapely hands in a constant state of flutter.

Then there was the Devil. Claude, a seedy gentleman wearing all black, who looked like every fairy tale's description of old Diabolus, his sullen face sharpened in every direction: a long hooked nose, chin speared to a goatee, pointed ears. Even his hair twisted and coiled into horns. His was a face made for derision. He smelled of tobacco and leathery cologne. Claude owned a publishing house in Paris.

Jean and I made up the table.

I immediately recognised Picasso's wife, Jacqueline, with her aristocratic profile and raven hair, from the innumerable portraits he'd painted of her. She came from the kitchen carrying a tray loaded with earthenware ramekins, which she handed out to each guest except for Picasso, who seemed content to nibble on raw carrots and sip Evian water. He introduced me to Jacqueline as 'Roast Beef' and we shook hands. As Jacqueline headed back to the house, he whispered to her briefly, then sniffed deeply and noisily at the garlicky aroma wafting from the ramekins.

"*Angula a la Bilbaína*," he purred. "Baby eels from the Sargasso Sea, caught in the river estuaries at Cadiz and Malaga."

I peered into the pot. The eels were tiny. They looked like a tangle of rubber bands. Funnily enough, they tasted like rubber bands too.

Jacqueline came back to the table, bringing a ten-gallon hat for Picasso. He stuck it on his head at a rakish angle. It was a gift from Gary Cooper, and he was particularly fond of wearing it. I was to find out during the evening that Picasso had a penchant for dressing up, particularly masks. Jacqueline had also brought a large white shirt, the old-fashioned collarless kind, which she insisted I wear, gesturing for me to remove my own sweaty shirt.

I put the dry shirt on. It was starched stiff as cardboard, and was so large it almost drowned me. But I instantly felt warmer.

"How droll," quipped Picasso. " Alan, you look like a choir boy. I bought that shirt in Paris after the war, 1947. I was going to wear it for the opening of *Oedipus Rex* at the Théâtre des Champs Elysées, dressed as a banker or Rothschild, but I thought people would misinterpret my gesture, saying I was flaunting my wealth. Particularly the Communists."

You could smell the next course, a pungent aroma of marine animals and fried onion, long before Jacqueline arrived and placed an enormous and shallow casserole at the centre of the table, accompanied by gastronomic growlings of approval from Picasso. What a dish. It was a veritable aquarium of dead sea creatures floating on a sea of gravy. Picasso pointed out gluey squid; cutlets of monkfish; halibut; sea bass; clams; gambas, pink as coral; Dublin Bay prawns like gargantuan fleas; slate-blue mussels; and a quartered lobster as red as a London bus. Jacqueline brought bottles of white wine and a large plate of lemon wedges, then joined us at the table.

"Zarzuela, King of Catalán – *suquet de peix* – fish stew," toasted Picasso, raising his glass of white wine.

"Zarzuela," we all responded, and for the next half-hour the conversation dwindled, as gambas got gulleted and mouths worked overtime, sucking and slurping meat from shells. We used bread to sponge and polish plates clean of the rich, brandied sauce, until nothing was left of the zarzuela, except neat little piles of shells, skin and bones. Even then, Picasso's restless imagination took these and laid them on his plate in a facial arrangement, finishing with a flourish by adding the antennae of the lobster as a moustache.

Beaming, he simply declared, "Dalí!" and we all applauded.

Picasso tilted his cowboy hat back on his head, folded his arms and smiled broadly. For a brief second he looked like Benito Mussolini.

I looked up at the full moon. Bats were out in force, inky silhouettes against the luminous saucer. Jacqueline brought out a tray of cheeses, gorgeous in their aromas. They looked like a drawer full of marvels from the British Museum: fossils or rare eggs from the Jurassic Period. No big slabs of cheddar here, but small palm-sized roundels of cheeses, some mottled green, brown-furred, blue-veined or creamy as duck eggs, all laid on vine leaves. A few of the cheeses still had labels affixed:

Bleu de Gex, Brie de Melun, Rogeret de chèvre, Brebis Pyrénées and two Queso de Burgos, drizzled with honey. Up until now, Picasso had repast sparingly, not eating the Angulas – I didn't blame him, they were awful! – and nibbling at the zarzuela, but the cheeses he attacked with gusto. He knew intimately the flavour and genealogy of each, encouraging everyone at the table to compare their distinctive tastes.

Coffee and brandy came and went. With everyone a little plumper, fitting tighter in their chairs, Diabolus, the publisher, announced it was his turn to create a *divertissement*, something to whet our imaginations. He handed notepaper and pencils to everyone, and instructed us to write no more than six words, any kind of sense or nonsense, whatever came immediately into our minds, then hand our contribution back to him and he would read them as a poem in random order.

"We will be amazed at the psychological revelations, personality bombshells it will expose."

Each of us scribbled our literary nuggets and passed them over to him. He put the slips of paper in his shirt pocket, pulled them out at random, and in a pompous voice as solemn as a church funeral, began to read.

"Baskets of eyeballs hang windward, as the coffin dropped down dead. And the angels snipped off their eyelids. Tannery-cured laceworks of human skin. The guitar makes dreams cry. Light is always on time. The blood of corpses is always sad."

Jean translated the poem with difficulty. It sounded like a load of old bollocks, but it invoked a firestorm of intellectual response. Animated arguments flared up and down the table among the guests, detonations of dispute, avid finger-pointing, much *merdes* and resorting to pantomime. The publisher, by far the most vocal, as if showing off his literary scholarship, flew into a Messianic diatribe which Jean was unable to translate, but it was dotted with words I understood: Freud, Pythagoras, Rama Krishna, Aquinas, schizophrenia and Gilles de Rais.

I sat and watched the lunatic performance. I noticed Picasso made no contribution to the farce but sat, arms folded across his chest, smiling benevolently. Finally, the publisher's argument fizzled to a few verbal squibs about the poet Verlaine, then silence.

Maurice, timing his response to perfection, addressed the publisher. "Monsieur, the truth is, you don't know your fucking arse from your elbow," he said, and then let out a long wavering fart. "And that's what I think of your diatribe poetique."

Everyone laughed so hard, tears rolled down most cheeks.

Things quieted down. Maurice asked Picasso if he would help him with his *divertissement* for the evening, a game of *exquisite corps*. Picasso sucked heavily on his Gitane, blowing out a thick cord of blue smoke, smiling in a way that folded his weathered face into concertinas of skin.

"Exquisite corpse," he replied, nodding enthusiastically. "A game invented by the surrealist André Breton in the thirties, who described it as 'the bewildered negation of the derisory activity of the imitation of physical aspects'."

In simpler terms, the game requires that three people, in turn, draw on a piece of paper folded in three, the head, body, and legs. Each part is drawn without the artist seeing the contribution of the others. When the paper is unfolded, it

reveals an exquisite corpse: a creature created by three, separate imaginations. The results are often startling in their originality. André Breton considered the finished drawings to be key to an artist's psychological profile.

Maurice drew the head, shielding his efforts with his hand, much like a kid hides his answers during an exam to prevent being copied. When he finished, he folded the paper so that the head was tucked out of sight, and passed it, with a pen, to Picasso. The second Picasso cheerfully began drawing, his face underwent a remarkable transformation: the years fell away, lines unlined, until he became childlike, his eyes wide with awe. He bent over the paper working studiously, flourishing the pen deftly; eighty-odd years old, he had no need for glasses. When he finished, Picasso folded his contribution out of sight and stared up and down the guests, considering each in turn with his big black eyes. A hush of expectation fell over the table. Who would want to follow Picasso?

He pushed pen and paper in front of me.

Maurice squealed. "Alan, you get to draw the legs and feet."

My mind went blank as the folded paper lay in front of me. I hadn't understood the discussion about exquisite corpses. Legs and feet where?

Picasso sensed my quandary. He pointed to two pen marks at the top of the fold. "The legs grow from here," he said.

I drew the first thing that came into my head, which I guessed was the psychological point of the exercise. A pair of legs playing soccer and, as an added silliness, I put faces on the kneecaps and handed the paper back to Maurice. He unfolded the drawing and held it up for everyone to see.

Maurice had drawn a frying pan with eggs and bacon that had an anthropomorphic quality; Picasso, a nude torso; I'd drawn a pair of bandy legs wearing soccer boots. The sum of the parts was incredibly funny and created quite a laugh. Unfortunately, the French just can't leave a good thing alone and so, yet again, Diabolus and Maurice got into a turgid intellectual debate.

Anxious to change the subject, Henri yelled above the argument. "So Alan, your *Le Salaire de la peur was magnifique*, your acting, it was *superbe*."

Acting? Nobody told me I was acting. Lord knew, I'd put one foot in the grave to get those bloody diamonds, scared shitless and peeing my pants to boot, all for some divertissement, whatever that was. Acting? I looked at Jean and he cringed. The bastard had set me up to perform some kind of charade. Only the stiff wad of money in my back pocket quelled my anger.

"Are you an actor?" questioned Maurice.

"No, I work on the docks, load and unload boats full of bananas," I replied, aware of what a pathetic occupation it was in the present company. Then I added, optimistically, "One of these days, though, I'm going to be an artist and do drawings."

I told them about my Uncle Sidney, his Rake's Progress, and my attempts at artistic entrepreneurship with the nudes.

"So what stops you becoming an artist?" asked Jacqueline.

I should have said fear, which would have been the truth, but I'd already built up a catalogue of reasons in my own head.

"Well, money," I began. "I get a few quid a week from the docks, most of which I spend on rent. I live with my aunt. I'd need to get a studio—"

Before I could continue my catalogue of woes, Picasso interrupted.

"You don't choose to be an artist, Alan," he said. "Art chooses you."

I didn't get a chance to respond to this monumental statement. I noticed signals being flashed between Jacqueline and Henri – tiny, almost imperceptible nods. Henri immediately stood up, flung his arms around Pablo and thanked the Picassos for a royal and wonderful night. As if on cue, everyone got up and said their gracious goodbyes. Apparently, Picasso was too polite to ever ask guests to leave, but those close friends of his at the table knew that Picasso was anxious to go to his studio by ten, and begin the lonely pursuit of painting. Most nights, he'd paint until dawn.

The Countess came over and told me she and Jean were heading to the casino in Nice to gamble, and they would love me to join them. The kinky bitch made my skin crawl. I felt embarrassed to be eyeball-to-eyeball with her, convinced she and Jean had got me drunk at the Carlton so that I could perform a few party tricks for the slag. Knowing Jean, the ponce had got well paid for my services. Still, if I could get to Nice with the tickle I had in my back pocket, maybe I could get a flight back to London.

I saw Picasso hurry into the house. A pity; I'd wanted to shake his hand and say goodbye. What a story I could brag about, over a few jars round the East End pubs. "Met Picasso, didn't I, had dinner with the geezer!" But the thought hit me: Tony and the boys would never have heard of Picasso. Brando, yeah, but Picasso? They'd think he made ice cream.

As all the guests were standing around saying their goodbyes, doing the 'If you're ever in Toulon, do drop in and see us' number, I had this idea for a right stroke I could've pulled during dinner. I'd have said to Picasso, "Mr Picasso, you invented Cubism, right?"

"In the early part of this century, I, along with several artists, helped in deconstructing the formal nineteenth century approach to painting," Picasso would've responded.

"Well see, Mr Picasso – and I quote from Bergerson's *The Psychoanalysis of Art* – 'Artists of the twentieth century paint from their inner paranoias, their phobias. Bocklin paints death; Van Gogh, the lunacy of ordinary objects; Delvaux, the virginal sphinx.' Your pursuit of Cubism, its denial of all circular forms, has prompted a substantial bet between Henri and myself."

"A bet?" Picasso cocked his head. "What sort of bet?"

"I bet Henri a hundred pounds, based on your obsession with Cubism, that you have square balls."

Picasso, along with everyone else at the table, looked shocked, aghast even. But Picasso just ain't the sort of bloke who shocks easy, and he started laughing.

"Square balls, Alan? I can assure you my balls are as round as Spanish onions. You lose the bet."

"Mr Picasso, I know you are a gentleman, a man of your word, but one hundred pounds is a small fortune for me. May I have proof that I've lost the bet?"

Picasso looked at me, then Jacqueline, then back to me, and unzipped the fly of his shorts. "Be my guest, but please don't squeeze the merchandise."

I put my hand inside his shorts, felt the Maestro's balls, weighed them carefully. They were round. I withdrew my hand.

"Henri, I lose the bet and owe you a hundred."

At that point, Jean pipes up. "Mr Picasso, Henri, I think we've been conned. Twenty minutes ago, Alan bet me five hundred pounds that, within the next half-hour, he could be coddling your balls, Maestro in his hands. He wins."

Everyone laughed. It's an old flanker. I wished I'd worked it during dinner. It would've been a nice little *divertissement.*

Picasso suddenly appeared back outside the house, cigarette and paintbrush in one hand, a palette dolloped with a variety of coloured oil paints in the other. Great, at least I might get an opportunity to shake his hand and say goodbye. He moved behind me. I heard him mention the Minotaur, then felt something clammy and sticky, like treacle, stripe down my back. This was followed by rapid pokes with something bristly. I heard the other guests gasp. I turned, anxious to find out what was happening and bumped into Picasso, crouched, grinning like an imp, bending behind me, painting my shirt.

"Turn round and be still," ordered Picasso.

Oh dear God, I'm being anointed in oils by the Master, the Midas of Art. I couldn't believe what was happening. The brush attacked like a swarm of insects, pounding and bouncing across my shoulders, poking, slashing up and down my arms, my spine, into my shoulders, all the time accompanied by 'oohs' and 'ahhs' from the onlookers. Picasso moved round to my front and continued painting, muttering almost imperceptibly in Spanish, emitting little grunts of satisfaction, his hand darting like a hummingbird from palette to shirt, fluttering the brush in swirling movements, daubing, spidering lines and cross-hatching, swooping ragged arcs of black paint, smearing on pinks, reds, tremulous yellow and aggressive greens.

For a full twenty minutes, Picasso circled me, spring-heeled, often up on his toes, a fencing master using his brush as a rapier, cutting, hacking, slicing his way to the final creation, no stopping for a second, until, finally, he stepped back and uncrouched, circled me to view his creation. He was flushed and breathing heavily.

"*C'est fini*," he said simply.

Everyone burst into applause and bravos. I stood, flushed with excitement, looking downward onto the shirt and trying to decipher the design, but couldn't. Picasso came and stood in front of me, shining those huge eyes into my face.

"Alan, the minotaur is for you. If you need money, take it to Kahnweiler in Paris. Tell him Picasso sent you. He'll give you a good price for it."

I was too dazed to say thank you. Guests wheeled around me, awed at the magic Picasso had just created, its power to bewitch – how he transformed a utilitarian object into a Minotaur breathing life.

Picasso took Jacqueline by the hand and the two of them walked into the house. The windows turned to darkness as the guests climbed into their cars. Headlights flaring, the vehicles slowly cruised down the drive towards the front gate, until I was left with just Jean, the Countess and the skull-coloured moon for company. Jean didn't want the wet oil paint on my shirt to ruin the leather interior of his car, so I took it off and lay it lovingly out in the trunk. The front showed a naked lady seeming to enjoy being ravished by a minotaur; on the back was a portrait, which I guessed was meant to be me, with fishes and a lobster, signed by Picasso with the words, "Pour le garcon avec la visage chat."

We drove to Mougins.

I wasn't going to mention the *Salaire de la peur caper*, happy to keep mum and hang onto the money, but Jean did anyway.

"Alan, the Salaire Charade – Henri Clouzot, the pipe-smoking gentleman – is an old friend of Picasso's. One of his most famous films is *Le Salaire de la peur, The Ways of Fear*. Picasso came up with the idea to act out the title. I should have told you it was just a party piece, but thought if you didn't know, the event became more... How shall I say? *Surréel*. We watched you enter the house from our various hiding places. All the others thought you were acting. You were brilliant. Oh, by the way, Alan, the money in your back pocket is fake, stage money. Don't try spending it."

The right bastard put me through ten minutes of heebie jeebies just for a charade, but I'd ended up with a shirt painted by Picasso and a night I could milk for years. But even so... What a liberty! One of these days, I thought, I'll have Jean's guts for garters.

We parked outside the village wall at the Saracens Gate. It was a rule in the East End, if you left anything in your car that could get nicked, it would get nicked. So I got the shirt out of the trunk and put it on. We wound our way through the narrow medieval streets, which, despite the late hour, were packed with tourists. We came out into a beautiful square,

Place de la Mairie, crowded with people drinking at bars, tossing coins into flower-decked fountains.

We went to Relais. The place was packed, but there was something imperious about the Countess. She parted people like Moses at the Red Sea, and, when the maître d' clocked her, he went immediately into bowing and scraping mode – like she was royalty – and whisked us to a table. The shirt, with its erotic design and brash colours, caused quite a stir. People began to press around the table, to stare at it and me. Some were clearly disgusted, snarling and spitting curses at me. I had to wonder, if the shirt were hung in an art gallery, whether it would evince the same vitriolic response? Others were curious. Was I a pop star? Was the shirt a new Paris fashion?

One morose gentleman, who lived in Mougins, said he thought it sacrilegious that I would wear a print of a Picasso painting on such a mundane object as a shirt. What were the youth of today coming to? Didn't we have any respect for the Arts? Unfortunately, the Countess, in a moment of indiscretion, countered, telling the man Picasso had painted the shirt as a gift for me, less than two hours earlier. The word Picasso got repeated by onlookers. Like a virus, it swept from throat to throat through the bar and out onto the streets. In no time at all, the crowd thickened to a mob, pushing and shoving dangerously around our table, taking photos, grabbing at the shirt while people at the entrance, thinking Picasso was dining, rubbernecked and shoved, desperate for a glimpse of the Maestro. In the chaos, tables got knocked over and people fell. Waiters had to push through the throng to rescue the Countess, escorting her to safety outside on the street. I couldn't see Jean in the confusion, so I fought my way against the tide of infatuants towards the rear exit. Customer jackets hung by the exit on coat racks. I grabbed one, pulled it on over the shirt and stepped into the street. I watched as the horde funnelled into the bar, yelling for Picasso.

It was a scene straight out of *Day of the Locusts.*

I hurried down to Saracens Gate. Jean's Bentley was still parked there, but I kept going. Somehow, I felt my voyage to the South of France was over. It was better to head to Paris, to Kahnweiler, and cash in my shirt. I walked in a state of euphoria along a country road, light-footed, as though lifted up by angels. The full moon gave the gloom a curious radiance, as it filtered through tall cypresses and the convoluted branches of olive trees. Across fields of lavender, wisps of fog drifted like gangs of phantoms. Far away, I could hear the dynamo hum of traffic.

After a twenty-minute walk, I reached a main highway, the N-85. Road signs showed Cannes to be five miles south, Grasse five miles north. I could head to Cannes and catch the train to Paris, but the undisciplined potential of hitchhiking north through Grasse appealed to the outlaw in me.

So I turned, thumb at the ready. I began the long trek to Paris, and from there I'd head back home to the smoke, where I would try my hand at the Art game.

and next …

In the sequel to *Pipe Dreams*, I'll be recounting my time with The Beatles and painting a vivid picture of those memorable years that defined my career.